GOLD RUSH COUNTRY

GUIDE TO CALIFORNIA'S MOTHER LODE & NORTHERN MINES

By the Editors of Sunset Books and Sunset Magazine

Lane Books · Menlo Park, California

Hydraulic nozzle at Forest Hill.

Second Printing July 1968

FOREWORD

The event that first focused on California the rapt attention of the rest of the world was, of course, Jim Marshall's finding of a few flakes of yellow metal in the tailrace of Captain Sutter's new sawmill beside the American River. What happened during the next half-dozen years forms one of the most dramatic chapters in the nation's history. For a horde of Argonauts, traveling by land and water, converged on California from all points of the compass, and in their ardent hunt for gold explored every nook and cranny of the Sierra foothills from Mariposa northward to Mount Shasta and beyond.

During their brief stay in the Mother Lode country, the gold hunters left an impress on the land that a full century has failed to erase. To be sure, during the hundred years that have elapsed since then, many changes have occurred. Some of the once populous early-day camps have disappeared entirely; the sites of others are marked only by heaps of rubble and a few ruined walls, while yet others have become prosperous towns, their streets lined with substantial modern buildings of brick or stone.

With this fine book on the arm of his comfortable chair or the seat of his moving car, the reader can better "travel through" the exciting past of the Gold Rush Country. It is in one volume a solid contribution to both Western travel literature and Californiana. For those who today venture into the area, whether by armchair or automobile, will find on its pages precisely that information, briefly and authentically set forth, that will enable them to understand and appreciate the abundance of historical lore that still clings to virtually every stream, every town, and every abandoned campsite. Without some such mentor, much of the romance of the region would surely be missed; with it, it becomes easy to seek out those relics of the past that enable one to visualize the stirring events which took place there a century or more ago.

Incidentally, it is altogether appropriate that this excellent guidebook to the Mother Lode country should have been compiled and issued by the publishers of *Sunset* Magazine. For *Sunset,* ever since its founding well over a half century ago, has devoted itself to chronicling the attractions of life in the West, and although it has been mainly concerned with the contemporary scene, from time to time it has turned backward to reveal to present-day readers some phase of the region's eventful past.

OSCAR LEWIS

ACKNOWLEDGMENTS

No book of this sort could have been written without the help of interested and qualified people—those who supplied raw material and later checked the rough manuscript. We are indeed indebted to many who have contributed their assistance.

We are particularly grateful for the help given by the following: John Hassler of Coloma; Alma Rowe of Mariposa; Carlo DeFerrari of Sonora; Margaret E. Lambert of Downieville; the staff of the California section of the California State Library; George O. Brooks of Nevada City; Clarke Stanley of Carmichael; Wallace L. Krill of Sacramento; Jim Oliver of the Tuolumne County Chamber of Commerce; Gertrude Waller of the Calaveras County Chamber of Commerce; Sid Smith of the Amador County Chamber of Commerce; Edward V. Brotherhood of the Placer County Chamber of Commerce; M. L. Good of the Grass Valley area Chamber of Commerce; Irene McMasters of the Nevada City Chamber of Commerce; L. Van Tongeren of the Oroville Chamber of Commerce.

PHOTOGRAPHERS

COVER PHOTOGRAPH, by Robert Cox, shows Columbia, one of two Gold Country towns that are preserved in state parks (the other is Coloma). Through restoration of old buildings, park officials hope to recreate a mining town of 1860.

WILLIAM BRONSON: 24 (r.), 39 (bottom), 42 (bottom), 55 (l.). CALIFORNIA HISTORICAL SOCIETY, SAN FRANCISCO: 91 (bottom). CALIFORNIA STATE LIBRARY: 12, 14, 20, 38 (r.), 52, 54, 56, 57 (top r.), 61 (l.), 63, 66 (bottom), 72, 77 (middle), 78 (bottom) 85. CLYDE CHILDRESS: 45 (bottom), 48 (r.). GLENN CHRISTIANSEN: 81 (bottom). BOB IACOPI: 2, 10, 13 (top l., bottom), 15 (top l., bottom), 26, 27, 28, 33 (top), 34, 35, 38, 39 (top), 41, 43 (top), 44, 45 (top r., bottom), 47 (bottom), 48 (top l., bottom), 53, 57 (l., bottom), 60, 64, 66 (top), 67, 68, 70, 73, 74, 75 (bottom), 77 (bottom), 79, 80, 81 (top), 82, 83, 87, 88, 90, 91 (top), 92. ROBERT COX: cover, 30 (top), 31 (bottom). RICHARD DAWSON: 81 (center). WALTER HOUK: 21 (bottom), 22 (bottom), 23 (bottom). ESTHER LITTON: 76. MARTIN LITTON: 13 (top r.), 15 (top r.), 17, 22 (top), 23 (bottom), 25 (top r.), 30 (bottom), 32 (top), 42, 46, 55 (bottom), 61 (top r.), 61 (bottom), 75 (top), 78 (top). JIM MARTIN: 40 (r.). SIDNEY SMITH: 47 (top). LEWIS W. STEWART: 36, 43 (bottom). TUOLUMNE COUNTY MUSEUM: 32 (bottom). DARROW M. WATT: 9 (bottom), 49.

CONTENTS

SPECIAL FEATURES

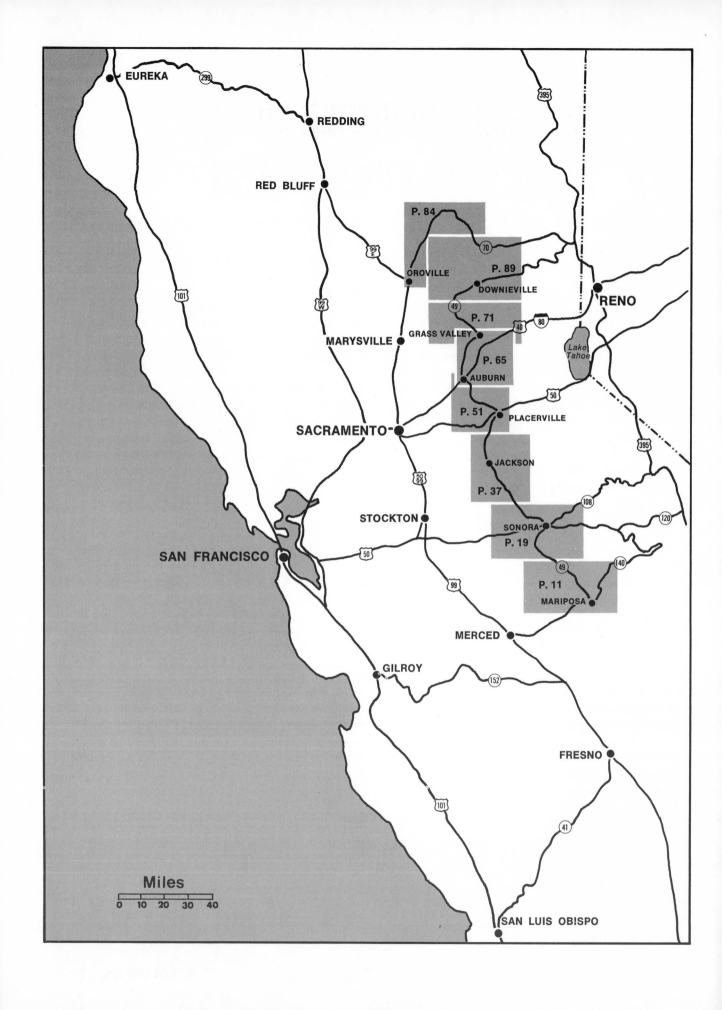

EUREKA

299

REDDING

RED BLUFF

99E

P. 84

70

OROVILLE

P. 89

DOWNIEVILLE

RENO

49

P. 71

99W

MARYSVILLE

GRASS VALLEY

40

80

Lake Tahoe

P. 65

AUBURN

50

P. 51

101

SACRAMENTO

PLACERVILLE

395

50 99

JACKSON

P. 37

108

120

STOCKTON

50

SONORA

P. 19

49

140

99

P. 11

MARIPOSA

SAN FRANCISCO

MERCED

GILROY

152

FRESNO

101

41

Miles

0 10 20 30 40

SAN LUIS OBISPO

INTRODUCTION TO
THE GOLD RUSH COUNTRY

"Monday 24th this day some kind of mettle was found in the tail race that looks like goald first discovered by James Martial, the boss of the mill."

With this innocent and barely legible entry in his diary, Henry W. Bigler recorded the moment in January, 1848, that changed the course of Western history and set hearts palpitating throughout the world. Henry Bigler was a workman at Sutter's sawmill in the California foothills, a virtually unexplored area in early 1848. Neither he nor James "Martial" realized that within a year the primitive territory of California would be known from Australia to Wales, and a great migration would be under way that would open the West.

"Forty-niners," they are often called in respect to the first big year of the California Gold Rush; but there were also '48ers and '53ers and many more who responded to the lure of gold. The dream of quick and easy riches had universal appeal, and men fairly drooled over the first stories that came out of California. Nuggets as big as your fists, just lying there on the ground to be picked up by passing strangers. Gravels so rich that a single panful could produce the fortune of a lifetime. Think of it — gold, as much as you wanted, waiting in the foothills of California.

The fact that mining in the Gold Rush country was miserable drudgery, filled with disappointments, does not seem to dull this glorious image. Those who worked knee-deep in icy water to dig out just enough gold to pay the astronomical prices of bed and board, or toiled long hours deep in a quartz mine, lost their naivete in a hurry. But the millions who learned about the Gold Rush only through second-hand stories and hand-me-down legends will always carry with them the image of the big strike, the free ride for life.

The great historical and economic importance of the California Gold Rush will keep it alive forever in the textbooks of our schools. But in our hearts, it is kept alive by its unique character and its unique characters. Extremes were the order of the day during the Gold Rush, and there are literally hundreds of stories that will never cease to cause modern men to shake their heads in wonder and disbelief.

This disbelief is sometimes justified, since many stories have a way of getting bigger and better with each retelling. Yet for each tall tale, there are a dozen real anecdotes that do not need the added frills of exaggeration. Towns really did grow up overnight and disappear almost as fast. It's true that miners once dug up a single gold nugget that weighed 195 pounds troy. During the early days, it was not unusual for a miner to pay a dollar for a slice of bread and another dollar to butter it. He paid $100 for a blanket, $100 for a horse, and $20 for a shovel with which to dig his fortune or his folly.

One of the saddest aspects of the Gold Rush Country is that there is so little left — so few *things* — to go with the stories of that wild and crazy time. Many of the gold mining camps were flimsy and temporary to begin with, and a century of harsh weather and human neglect has taken its toll. The California Division of Mines and Geology estimates that 500 towns were born in the Gold Rush Country between 1848 and 1860. Far more than half of these settlements are completely gone. Of the remainder, a big percentage are little more than names on signposts. Only a handful managed to thrive after the gold was gone and adapt themselves to the twentieth century.

CHANGE IS INEVITABLE

Even since the first edition of this book was published in 1957, there have been some notable changes. A fire has taken a good many of Jamestown's handsomest old wooden buildings; new highway alignment has erased the last remains of Mormon Bar; the waters of the Merced River have drowned Bagby; a new freeway has knifed through Nevada City. More changes are inevitable: In the early 1970's, Jacksonville will disappear under the waters of the reservoir behind the new Don Pedro Dam; Grass Valley's traffic congestion will be relieved by a new freeway that is sure to destroy some of the gold mining sites; who knows where the next fire will strike? Weather, too, works against the old adobe and stone structures. Buildings crumble a little more with each winter, until they finally collapse or are washed down to the foundations.

There are a few bright spots. Chambers of commerce and organized citizens' groups work mightily to save the old buildings and preserve at least some of the old-time atmosphere. Fortunately, there have been some notable successes. Private enterprise lends a helping hand on occasion; some of the new banks and other commercial buildings are being painstakingly constructed in the finest tradition of authentic Gold Rush architecture and make very handsome additions to the old mining towns.

This book covers the area on the western slopes of the Sierra Nevada between Mariposa and Sattley that was the main mining center during the Gold Rush. Many historians divide this area into the Mother Lode — Mariposa to Auburn — and the Northern Mines. Others divide it into the Northern, Central, and Southern mines. But for general purposes, the whole region can be regarded as a single entity. This is by no means all of the gold-bearing land in California. It doesn't include the rich diggings around Weaverville, the Bodie area, or even the spot in the Southern California hills where gold was first discovered. But the Gold Rush Country considered here was the major gold belt and the scene of most of the action.

HIGHWAY 49 — PATH TO ADVENTURE

The Gold Rush Country fortunately is traversed by a good state highway, appropriately numbered State Route 49. You can see a good many of the major mining camps just by staying on this one highway. It's hard to resist the side roads, though, for it is here that you will find the little out-of-the-way towns that often reflect more of the Gold Rush atmosphere than the bigger towns along Highway 49.

Not all of Highway 49 is pretty. The outskirts of some of the larger towns, for example, were not planned for sightseers. But the brief passages of ugliness are forgotten when you hit the country-lane stretch between Cool and Pilot Hill, or the spectacular switchbacks between Bear Valley and Coulterville.

The Gold Country ranges in altitude from rolling grassland a few hundred feet above sea level to the 6,700-foot elevation of fir-clad, often snowy Yuba Pass. State Route 49 stays at around 2,000 feet, except where it dips into the deep river canyons and where it climbs the mountains above Downieville. In summer, weather is likely to be fiercely hot at the lower levels but much more pleasant in the pine belt. Dust will probably be deep on the unpaved logging roads and on the trees beside them, just as it was along the thoroughfares traveled by the Concord coaches during the 1850's.

When fall arrives, the first rains settle the dust and wash the oaks, poplars, locusts, and eastern maples in time for them to brighten the old towns with yellow and vermilion. In winter, rain turns the red foothill soil to mud and snow covers the higher altitudes. Touring can still be a pleasure, though, and many of the old ruins look better in the rain than they do under the dust and withering heat of August.

At the lower elevations, spring comes along early in February and March. La Porte still may have some snow in April or May, but the rest of the foothills are green with new grass and colorfully dotted with wildflowers. As the days grow longer, you'll find mile on mile of blazing Scotch broom, and fields of lupine, owl's clover, Mariposa lily, buttercup, brodiaea, and the glorious California poppy.

BIG TOWNS OR SMALL?

There is some dispute whether you'll find more of the Gold Rush atmosphere in the little deserted ghost towns or the bigger cities that still teem with activity. The decaying settlements have a timeless quality about them and there is great charm in the old ruins, particularly if you can explore and photograph them when early-morning or late-afternoon light casts long shadows among the crumbling adobe walls and rusty iron shutters.

On the other hand, the big towns like Sonora or Jackson or Grass Valley more closely resemble life in the Gold Rush days than do the sleepy ghost towns. The crowds that fill the shop-lined streets in these noisy, bustling communities are more like the lively crowds that thronged the camps in an earlier day. There may be little of picturesque quality left on the main streets, but of course there was nothing picturesque about the old town in the eyes of those who lived there a century ago. Some of the good-sized towns have two faces: the main street is busy and modern, but the side streets are still narrow and crooked and lined with old houses and stores that are closer to the Gold Rush than they are to the 1960's.

MUCH INFORMATION IS AVAILABLE

Probably nowhere is data dispensed so generously and enthusiastically as in this tradition-proud land. It's easy to become well informed on the Gold Rush, and if authorities sometimes conflict on dates or the validity of one story or another, they generally agree on most things.

The California Division of Highways, various historical societies, and the Native Sons and Daughters of the Golden West have erected scores of markers throughout the countryside, and you can get a good idea about the area just by reading these alone. Museums—good ones—are everywhere and generally worth your time. There are also a number of gift stores and antique shops where you can buy authentic artifacts, second-hand junk, and even raw gold. Chambers of commerce are very active, and you can get loaded down with maps and printed guides just for the asking.

Your public library can also provide a great deal of information, and the gold regions will mean much more after you've sampled some of the absorbing literature that the land and its people have inspired. The stories of Mark Twain and Bret Harte are well-known. Some of the quietest rural landscapes come to rollicking life with Joseph Henry Jackson's *Anybody's Gold*. And winding down to nondescript Rich Bar after sampling the *Shirley Letters* is like going home.

Some of the old things require no literary build-up. It's enough, for instance, just to stand in the Mariposa County courthouse and know that it has remained virtually unchanged since the days when John C. Fremont fought many legal battles to hold on to his vast empire.

HOW TO USE THIS BOOK

The chapters of this book are based on arbitrary division of the Gold Rush Country, but each section centers around at least one major town where you will find accommodations. Every section would take at least a full weekend to cover if you plan to do anything more than merely drive through the old towns. But as convenient as the divisions are from this standpoint, don't attach any historical or geographical importance to the lines that we have drawn, unless, of course, they happen to be county lines, too.

On the opening pages of each chapter, you will find a detailed road map that will help you find your way to all of the towns mentioned in the text. The towns are not discussed in any strict geographical order, but rather in the order you might encounter on a motoring trip driving from south to north. The routes followed are, of course, only representative of many you might want to plan.

If you want to set a record, you can probably drive the 270 twisting miles of Highway 49 between Mariposa and Sattley in a day, but you won't see much and your tires and temper will surely suffer. A long weekend will let you pause at the markers and absorb a smattering of lore, with no time out for picture-taking. You can make a pretty thorough reconnaissance of Highway 49 in a week, but you would need twice as much time to include the side trips without which some of the most meaningful things are missed.

With patience and determination, modern miners can still pan a few flakes of gold from Gold Country streams.

There's plenty of gold on display in the old towns; these boys are examining nuggets in a Coulterville museum.

ERECTED 1854

MARIPOSA COUNTY
COURT HOUSE

California's oldest courthouse is still in service at Mariposa. It has remained virtually unchanged since the doors were first opened in 1854, seven years before the inauguration of Abraham Lincoln.

THE MARIPOSA AREA

MARIPOSA • MOUNT BULLION • MOUNT OPHIR • HORNITOS
BEAR VALLEY • COULTERVILLE • LA GRANGE

Mariposa

Mariposa is the most southerly town of any historical importance in the Mother Lode, and it makes a good anchor for State Route 49. The community has managed to preserve several Gold Rush buildings, and it has an excellent historical center and museum with good displays and some knowledgeable hosts who can help travelers find points of interest throughout the county.

Mariposa is far from a ghost town. It has a small, stable farming base, and the business district also gets a sizable amount of tourist traffic because of its convenient position halfway between Merced and Yosemite National Park. But the old buildings are not hard to find. Right on the main street are the Trabucco warehouse and store, the I.O.O.F. Hall, and the balconied

Schlageter Hotel which has been converted into stores and office space.

One block east of the main street is the old stone jail, once the largest jail in the entire Mother Lode. The 30 by 50-foot granite block structure has not been out of service for too many years, and it looks just as sturdy as ever.

The choicest architectural morsel in Mariposa is above the commercial section on a quiet hill at the north end of town. The two-story wooden courthouse, the oldest in the state, has been in continuous use since 1854 and has been recognized as one of the Mother Lode's finest buildings since the day it opened. The only change in its countenance came in 1967 when the belfry had to be strengthened and slightly remodeled. The building's classically simple lines and stark white

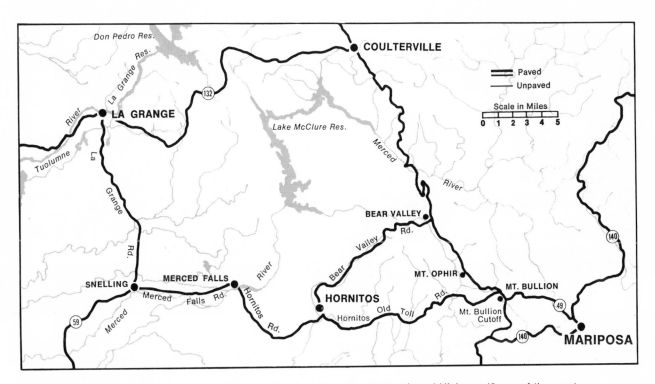

Spectacular switchbacks between Bear Valley and Coulterville make this section of Highway 49 one of the most scenic drives in the Gold Rush Country. Wildflowers are plentiful along side roads in early spring.

THE FICKLE FORTUNES OF JOHN C. FREMONT

John C. Fremont was one of those who didn't make it in the California gold fields. In the 1850's, he had great national prestige, enough gold-producing lands to guarantee ten fortunes, and a bright political future. But he blew the whole thing, and wound up a man beset by financial and legal troubles beyond all reasonable limits.

Fremont was born in 1813 and spent a very busy early life. By the time gold was discovered in California, this illegitimate son of a French teacher and a high-born Virginia lady had married the daughter of popular U. S. Senator Thomas Hart Benton; done some excellent topographic mapping of Missouri River territory; traveled the Rockies with Kit Carson; made an unauthorized trip into California with a 12-pound howitzer in tow; and led the first winter crossing of the Sierra Nevada.

He was very active in the fight to wrest California from Mexico, and even though many of his actions were taken without official sanction, he emerged as a popular hero. But Fremont's fortunes took a bad turn when he backed the wrong man in the struggle between Commodore Robert Stockton and General Stephen Kearny over military leadership of the new territory. Stockton rewarded Fremont's allegiance by appointing him governor and commander-in-chief of the armed forces in California in January, 1847. But the honor came to naught as Kearny took over command from Stockton and promptly ordered Fremont's court martial.

Back in Washington, Fremont was found guilty of disobeying orders (Kearny's) and ordered out of the military service. President Polk remitted the penalty, but Fremont had no choice but to resign.

It was about this time that Fremont accidentally became the largest single owner of gold-bearing property in the world. Before leaving for his court martial in February, 1847, Fremont gave his agent, Thomas Larkin, $3,000 and instructions to buy an attractive piece of land near Mission San Jose where civilian John C. Fremont could retire in peace. But for some still-unexplained reason, Larkin instead bought 45,000 acres of hot, dry land in the Sierra foothills for Fremont, and bought the Mission San Jose property for himself.

Fremont was livid, but could do nothing except go to Washington for his trial. After the court martial, redemption, and resignation, Fremont started back to California and en route found that gold had been discovered on his foothill land. When he realized the extent of the gold findings, the crafty ex-soldier took fortune firmly by the scruff of the neck and "floated" his original purchase up into the hills to take in even more gold-producing land, most of which had already been claimed by others. This gave him a single piece of property extending from the Merced River south to Bridgeport — an L-shaped chunk some 17 miles long and 5 miles wide at its greatest dimensions.

With this wealth behind him, Fremont — now 45 years old — moved into the political forefront and became one of California's leading citizens. He was named U. S. Senator before California was a state, and then went to Washington to campaign for admission. When statehood

Young Fremont, before the fall.

was granted, Fremont served briefly as senator, and became the first Presidential candidate of the fledgling Republican party in 1856. But he was beaten by Buchanan, and his career started downhill.

The next crushing blow came when Fremont's very influential father-in-law died. Then, in 1857, Fremont returned to his Mariposa land and found that absentee ownership, bad management, and costly lawsuits filed by miners who had been uprooted by Fremont's "floating" land grab were eating up all of the tremendous profits from the mining. The California courts ultimately ruled that Fremont's expanded holdings were valid, but the nefarious scheme had earned him some bad enemies, many of whom tried to make trouble for the landholder.

Fremont built a mansion at Bear Valley and settled down to enjoy the good life with his family and personally supervise his huge empire for a time. But strange things continued to happen in the accounting department. The mines produced at a record-breaking rate, but there were no profits. Tremendous overhead costs for the mining operations, personal expenses, and legal involvements were eating up all the cash. Finally, in 1861, Fremont decided to go to Europe to raise more cash. But the Civil War intervened, and the old soldier abandoned his personal affairs to return to public life. This was a tragic mistake.

Fremont's very controversial military campaigning and his political foolhardiness in opposing Abraham Lincoln cost him his military commands, his political influence, and finally his public prestige. Without new capital, finances at the Mariposa land went from bad to worse. Finally, in 1863, the property had to be sold for a fraction of its worth. Fremont received enough from the sale to live comfortably, but he managed to lose it all through unwise railroad speculations during the next decade. He died penniless in 1890 in New York.

During the midst of his financial crises at Mariposa, Fremont once said "When I came to California I hadn't a cent; now I owe two million dollars." That may have been true, but this great explorer gave much of himself to California. The Mariposa mines pumped millions of dollars into the economy, and continued to produce into the twentieth century. And Fremont himself can scarcely be forgotten by future generations — his name has been given to more streets, towns, peaks, and landmarks than any other pioneer in Western history.

Crumbling ruins of a Trabucco store are all that remain of Mount Ophir, site of California's first private mint.

Built in 1862, St. Joseph's Catholic Church still stands on a prominence above the south end of Mariposa.

walls never fail to impress visitors, and there are no plans for moving the county offices for quite some time. The courtroom still has many of its original furnishings. The original clock in the tower has tolled out the hours since 1866.

Mariposa ("butterfly" in Spanish) was once part of the 46,000 acre tract belonging to John C. Fremont (see page 12). It has served as seat of Mariposa County since 1852.

The Mariposa Mine near the south end of town, discovered by Kit Carson and Alex Gody in 1849, supplied the first steam quartz mill in California. (You can see the entrance to the mine from the back of St. Joseph's Catholic Church.) Gold production continued into the twentieth century and actually hit its peak between 1900 and 1915.

Mount Bullion

As with so many town sites along the Gold Country roads, there is little left at Mount Bullion to suggest the fevered activity of the 2,000 men who first worked the placers in 1850 and then turned to the rich quartz veins in their search for gold. The now-vanished Princeton Mine, which produced more than $4 million, was located just south of the present town site.

Balconied Schlageter Hotel is a good example of Gold Rush architecture; high sidewalks characterize old towns.

Fanciful "portrait" ignores reality.

THE MURIETA MADNESS

Joaquin Murieta was the most romantic figure of the California Gold Rush. Immortalized in books, paintings, innumerable anecdotes, and even a Hollywood motion picture, Murieta emerged as Robin Hood of the Southern Mines, avenger of his murdered family, friend of the poor, and defender of his countrymen.

The legend of Joaquin Murieta is still very much alive. Visitors to the Gold Country will find his name inscribed on historical markers and plaques, and his heroic feats recounted endlessly by old timers. Saw Mill Flat outside of Sonora claims to be the place where Murieta first settled when he arrived from Sonora, Mexico, in 1850. It was in Murphys that the handsome young man allegedly swore vengeance against his Yankee persecutors after they tied him to a tree and beat him bloody, then ravished his wife and murdered his brother.

Residents of San Andreas tell how a Frenchman made Murieta's famous bulletproof vest, and then had to prove its effectiveness by wearing it while Joaquin shot at him from point blank range. In Hornitos, there is an underground tunnel supposedly used by the bandit to escape hotly-pursuing lawmen. Outside of Volcano, there used to be a well-disguised treehouse where Joaquin is said to have hidden while puzzled rangers milled around beneath him. Mokelumne Hill, Sonora, and a dozen other towns claim to be the scenes of Murieta's wild escapades.

According to the legend, Murieta died in a blaze of glory in 1853. He was hunted down by a lawman named Harry Love and shot dead in southern Mariposa County. Love cut off the bandit's head, put it in a bottle of alcohol, and used it as proof to claim a state reward.

How much of this legend is true? That depends on your point of view. Tellers of tales swear that it's all true. Local residents usually smile and admit that maybe a few of the details have been fabricated. Some historians accept only part of the legend. Other historians, notably Joseph Henry Jackson, claim that it's all a fairy tale, one of the most outlandish packs of lies ever put together. In his book *Bad Company,* and in other writings, Jackson has applied a very sharp scalpel to the Murieta legend and carefully traced its origins to the flowery pens of imaginative authors.

There are a few facts involved, but not many. In 1852 and 1853, the Southern Mines were bothered by a number of thieves, all named Joaquin. There was Joaquin Valenzuela, Joaquin Carrillo, Joaquin Murieta, Joaquin Botilleras, and a few others — all villains. With so many similarly-named bandits committing so many crimes, it was hard to pin down just which Joaquin actually did what to whom.

Authorities arriving at the scene of a crime would ask, "Who did it?" Most often, the answer was simply "Joaquin."

In response to public outcries, the state legislature really did hire Harry Love in May, 1853, to go get a bandit named Joaquin — no last name specified — and dangled $5,000 as the carrot in front of the lawman's nose. Love took the job but didn't have much luck for several weeks. Finally he surprised a group of Mexicans around their campfire one night and killed a few, including a man who claimed to be their leader but who never mentioned his name. Love decapitated the man, named him Joaquin Murieta out of desperation, and went back to claim his reward.

The legislature paid off, but not everyone was convinced of the head's identity. A surviving member of the Mexican gang claimed that it belonged to Joaquin Valenzuela. Some of Murieta's supposed "relatives" were brought forth by authorities to identify the deceased. But others who knew Joaquin Murieta claimed that the grisly prize bore no resemblance to the man.

It was about a year after this confusion died down that the legend of Joaquin Murieta was born, according to Jackson. A not-too-successful writer named John Rollin Ridge dreamed up a book called *The Life and Adventures of Joaquin Murieta, the Celebrated California Bandit.* Ridge made up the whole wild story, including many of the details now accepted as fact, and then cleverly ended the sordid tale by having the criminal killed and decapitated by Harry Love. The public knew that Love had actually killed a Mexican bandit, so it chose to believe that the rest of the story was based on fact.

During the next century, the Murieta legend was revived many times, with each new writer basing his research not on fact, but on Ridge's fairy tale. With each retelling, a few new details were added. Over the years, Joaquin grew even handsomer, was able to trace his lineage to Montezuma, and displayed some new tricks that he had learned from a friend named Kit Carson.

"Portraits" were drawn, and even though most of the artists admitted that their work was pure fiction, the public accepted the drawings as actual likenesses.

On the basis of the historical revelations, the myth of Joaquin Murieta should be cast down as hokum. And those who debunk the legend must debunk all the stories, the monuments, and even some of the history books. There is no middle ground. This is not so easy to do. The Gold Rush needs a romantic hero, and the mythical Murieta fills the need. History notwithstanding, it seems certain that the legendary Joaquin Murieta will not die — or even suffer a serious illness — for a long time to come.

Hollow shells of Bear Valley buildings are gradually losing the battle against wind, rain and neglect.

Church buttressed in stone is one of several picturesque buildings that still stand in sleepy Hornitos.

Mount Ophir

The site of Mount Ophir is marked by stone ruins along a stretch of the old highway that parallels the present route of Highway 49 north of Mount Bullion.

It was at Mount Ophir in the early 1850's that John L. Moffatt operated the first private mint in California blessed with official authorization of the United States government.

Hornitos

This once roaring, lawless town is one of the most rewarding stops in the Mother Lode. Not only are there several old buildings still standing around the Mexican-style plaza, but the town is rich in history and colorful anecdotes. Hornitos was considered one of the rowdiest towns ever spawned during the Gold Rush, and it supposedly was the favorite haunt of Joaquin Murieta, certainly the most storied outlaw of early California (see page 14).

Founded by Mexican miners who had been "voted" out of neighboring Quartzburg by a law-and-order committee of Americans, Hornitos reflects Mexican influence more than any other Gold Country settlement. The town's name means "little ovens" in Spanish, and presumably was named after the little oven-shaped

In its heyday, Hornitos had a crowded business district that supplied hundreds of miners working in the area.

The little steam engine on display in Coulterville once was used to haul ore at the nearby Mary Harrison Mine.

Old walls of Jeffery Hotel in Coulterville are three feet thick. Ruins of another hotel are across the street.

tombs that the first settlers built above the ground for the dead. Some of these unusual graves can still be seen in a special little graveyard that has been fenced off below St. Catherine's Catholic Church (built in 1862).

The most noticeable ruin is that of the Ghirardelli Store, which was the starting point for the man who eventually was to build an empire based on chocolate. Nearby are the only one-story Masonic Lodge in the Gold Country, Gagliardo Store, Olcese Building, and other business establishments—some of which still carry bullet holes from miners' gun battles.

According to a local report, one of the adobes on the west side of the main street at the north end of town was an opium den of considerable disrepute. The town's museum is located in an old adobe building.

Murieta was such a common visitor to the wild old town that he was supposed to have had his own secret tunnel as an escape route from the fandango hall when the circumstances got too hot above ground. The entrance is now clearly marked at the corner of High Street and Bear Valley Road. In contradiction to this colorful legend is the more practical contention that the tunnel actually was used to roll beer barrels from a stable to the basement of the dance hall.

Hornitos' reputation for wildness has been enhanced by stories like that of the two gamblers (one version says they were women fandango dancers) who wrapped shirts (or shawls) around their arms as shields and duelled with gleaming knives in a vacant lot until they killed each other before a cheering audience of miners.

But the tragic tale of the Chinese, who in a moment of rage fired a pistol to frighten a tormenting white boy and by accident slightly wounded him, is one which few stories still told in the Gold Country can match.

The Chinese figured that his chances would be best if he headed for the hills, but he was soon caught by a posse and escorted to the Hornitos jail. Angry miners realized that it would be difficult, if not impossible, to break into the vault-like building, so with grisly ingenuity they lured the pitiful prisoner to the cell's tiny window with the promise of tobacco, then seized him, threw a noose around his neck and, by violently jerking the rope, literally dashed his brains out against the stone wall.

Incidentally, Quartzburg failed to survive despite its self-righteousness (or perhaps because of it). The now-abandoned town site is about three miles east of Hornitos on the Bear Valley Road.

Bear Valley

The few buildings left in Bear Valley don't speak of the days when General Fremont "owned" the town and ruled his sizable empire from the beautiful mansion he built for his wife and children, nor of the 3,000 souls who lived in the little city when local quartz was yielding gold in abundance.

The ruins that still sit beside the highway include the Bon Ton Saloon, a boarding house, the Garbarino Store, local I.O.O.F. Hall, and Trabucco Store. The roofless jail is on top of a small hill east of town. Unfortunately, there are no signs of the Fremont mansion or of the famed Oso House, a balconied hostelry built in 1850 of lumber brought around the Horn.

Immense piles of tailings cover the river banks near LaGrange. These were left by slow-moving dredgers.

You can catch a glimpse of the Mother Lode quartz formations through the trees west of Highway 49, about two miles south of Bear Valley. Two miles north of the town is a highway pull-out that affords excellent views of the Merced River. About halfway between Bear Valley and the Merced River Bridge are the buildings of the Pine Tree Mine, one of John Fremont's most disputed holdings. In 1967, historians exploring the scrub-covered hillsides west of this mine found what is believed to be the crumbling foundations of Fremont's "fort," built in the 1850's to help defend his mining empire against encroachment.

Coulterville

Coulterville was originally called Banderita, then Maxwellville; the official name was affixed after George W. Coulter set up store in a tent at the site in 1849. When Coulter arrived there was a sizable Mexican and Chinese population, but as in many other camps and towns in the mining country, Americans put all their prejudices to work and the "furriners" were expelled.

The Jeffery Hotel, which is the town's most imposing structure, is neither stately nor preposterous in appearance, but just about halfway between. The building was converted by George Jeffery in 1870 from a Mexican structure of rock and adobe built in 1851. The old walls are three feet thick. The saloon next door contains a small museum.

Across the street are the remains of the Coulter Hotel and the Wells Fargo Building that served as a trading post during the boom days when there were 25 saloons on the main street. Nelson Cody, the brother of Buffalo Bill, operated the business in the Wells Fargo Building during the 1870's and also served as postmaster for a time.

In front of these buildings are the local "hangin' tree" and a small steam engine that was used at the Mary Harrison mine north of town to haul ore along a stretch of track known as the world's crookedest railroad. You can still see part of the boiler house and foundation of this famous old mine that was opened in the 1860's and produced until 1903; drive south out of Coulterville on Highway 49 and turn right on the first black-topped road (about a mile from town). The mine shaft was once 1200 feet deep, with 15 levels and 15 miles of drift (side tunnels).

At one time, there was a sizable Chinese population in Coulterville. One Chinese adobe, the Sun Sun Wo Store, can still be found among the scattered residences east of town.

Coulterville has been gutted by three fires. The last blaze indirectly caused the village's last and perhaps the country's shortest "Gold Rush." In 1899, rubble of a stone-and-adobe building that was razed after the conflagration was used to fill chuckholes in the street. Apparently unknown to anyone living was a secret cache of gold coins in the very walls being used for fill. With the first rain, several of these coins were exposed by the running water and the rush was on. As the story goes, the town's populace turned out armed with shovels, picks, butcher knives, spoons, and other improbable mining tools, and quickly reduced the street to a state of impassable confusion.

La Grange

The picturesque village of La Grange is on the banks of the Tuolumne River, flanked by immense tailing piles that testify to the heavy mining activity that characterized the area for more than half a century.

The town was settled in 1852 by a group of French miners, and was logically named French Bar. When the gold gave out on the bar, the center of activity was moved up the hill, and commerce replaced the pick and shovel. There was a population of about 5,000 at the town's business peak, and La Grange even served as seat of Stanislaus County from 1855 to 1862. Three major stage lines made regular stops.

There are only a few Gold Rush buildings left in town. Near the east end of the present business district is a large stone building and the remains of the old adobe post office (now incorporated into a barn). At the opposite end of town is the wooden I.O.O.F. Hall.

Giant steam engine outside the Angels Camp museum was used for many years in the Calaveras County lumber industry. Angels Camp was one of the busiest boom towns in the Southern Mines.

THE SONORA AREA

PRIESTS • BIG OAK FLAT • GROVELAND • SECOND GARROTE • JACKSONVILLE

CHINESE CAMP • STENT • QUARTZ • KNIGHTS FERRY • COPPEROPOLIS

ALTAVILLE • ANGELS CAMP • CARSON HILL • JACKASS HILL • TUTTLETOWN

RAWHIDE • SHAWS FLAT • SPRINGFIELD • COLUMBIA • SONORA

JAMESTOWN • VALLECITO • DOUGLAS FLAT • MURPHYS

Priests

Priests—originally known as Kirkwood's or "Rattlesnake House" in the early 1850's — has nothing of historical interest to offer today, but at one time it was a key stopover for travelers to Yosemite Valley and an important supply base for miners in the area. The famous Priest Hotel, with its excellent food and spectacular seven-county view, enjoyed world-wide fame for several decades; but fire long ago took the last remainder of the once-proud structure.

Big Oak Flat

The gold-laden gravels that made Big Oak Flat a rich placer camp were discovered late in 1849 by James Savage, whose company included five Indian wives and several Indian servants. This is the same Savage who discovered Yosemite Valley a year later while leading a group of volunteers in pursuit of less friendly Indians.

The abundance of stone and adobe ruins found today in Big Oak Flat is far out of proportion to the present size of the village, and it is not difficult to

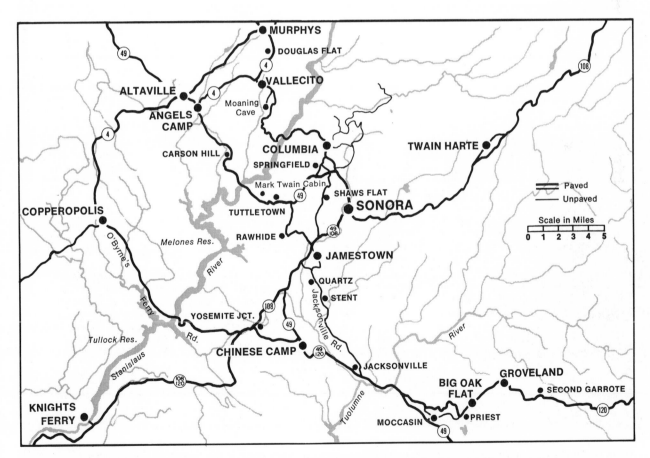

Some of the best towns in this area are on side roads. The drive between Columbia and Murphys takes you through beautiful mountain country. Jacksonville will be drowned by a new dam in the early 1970's.

BRET HARTE AND MARK TWAIN—THE WESTERN YEARS

Bret Harte and Mark Twain are the most famous and most popular of the many writers who have used the California Gold Rush for inspiration, background, and characters. They were among the first to recognize the unique qualities of the people, places, and events that were part of the Gold Rush, and their writings did as much to inform the world of this phenomenon as any history book ever could.

Strangely enough, neither man spent much time in the mines. But their brief exposure to the Western frontier had a lasting impression on both men, and they were able to draw on their California experiences for decades to come.

Bret Harte was only 12 years old and living in New York when gold was discovered at Coloma in 1848. He came to California in 1854, not in search of treasure, but to join his mother who had married a Colonel Andrew Williams of San Francisco after her first husband (and Bret's father) died in 1850. The reunited family settled down in Oakland, but young Bret yearned for new adventure. So he started for the foothills.

Harte arrived in the Southern Mines in 1855, when the first flush of the Gold Rush was already over and many of the mining camps were disintegrating. He taught school for a time in LaGrange, and then moved on to Robinson's Ferry on the Stanislaus River, where he was welcomed by superstitious miners who believed that a tenderfoot always brought good luck. Harte quickly acquired some partners, and they mined haphazardly for a few weeks, moving as far north as Angels Camp. He eventually wound up at the cabin on Jackass Hill owned by the Gillis Brothers, who paid for his stagecoach trip back to San Francisco. Bret returned to his stepfather's home and never again returned to the mines.

By his own admission, Bret Harte never really got to know the towns or the people intimately during his short stay in the Gold Rush Country. He was always the dude, wearing boiled shirts and patent leather shoes, and standing away from the intimacies of mining life. He didn't like the Sierra and once wrote that the foothills were "hard, ugly, unwashed, vulgar, and lawless."

After his trip to the mines, Harte embarked on a successful career as printer, newspaperman, magazine editor, and writer. His future was assured in 1860 with the publication of *M'liss*, the first of his mining stories. Shortly after that, Jessie Benton Fremont took a liking to him, and not only helped develop his talent but also got him a series of soft government jobs that paid his bills so he could have more free time for writing.

Harte eventually became the leading man of letters on the Pacific Coast and went East to capitalize on his fame, abandoning California forever. But he never turned his back on the West as a subject for his writing, and many of his best stories — even those written when he was living in England after 1885 — dealt with frontiersmen and life in the mining towns.

Samuel Clemens was born in Missouri in 1835 — a year before Bret Harte — but did not arrive in the West

Bret and Mark—portraits from the early years.

until 1861. By that time, he had served as newspaperman, printer, Mississippi River pilot, and even a Confederate soldier for two weeks at the start of the Civil War. He left the East to accompany his brother Orion, the newly-appointed governor of the Nevada territory. Young Sam tried prospecting both in Nevada and California's Humboldt County, then worked as city editor of the Virginia City Enterprise, where he first used the name of Mark Twain in 1862.

The young writer moved to San Francisco in 1864, and there met Bret Harte, who was a great help in getting Twain stories published and in improving the author's style.

In December, 1864, Twain visited the Gillis boys who had been kind to Bret Harte a few years earlier. They tried pocket mining for a time, and spent a lot of time in Angels Camp during the inclement weather. It was on a cold January day that Twain heard an old Mississippi River pilot named Ben Coon relate a funny anecdote about a frog jumping contest. A few months later, Twain wrote "The Celebrated Jumping Frog of Calaveras County" and became an overnight literary sensation. The next year, he left California and never returned.

In addition to the frog story, Mark Twain also collected enough other material in the mining country to last him for many years. He made a point to learn the miner's habits and his trade. He once said: "I know the mines and miners interiorly as well as Bret Harte knows them exteriorly." There was the major difference between the two. Harte had a genius for the narrative, and could capture character and local color in just a few words. But his stories lacked depth, and were those of an outsider. Twain, on the other hand, wrote like he talked — with a vitality that more truly reflected the California frontier and the rough people who settled it.

Born but a year apart, the two voices of the West died within two years of each other. Twain was in Connecticut when the end came in 1900, and Harte was in England when he died in 1902. Both had made an original contribution to the world of literature, and some of their best work was the direct result of short and very important visits to the California gold fields.

imagine the extent of the boom town that developed after Savage's discovery.

Groveland

Groveland was originally called Garrote, in honor of the hanging of a horse thief that took place in 1850. The name Groveland first appeared in the 1870's and presumably was chosen by a calmer populace.

The building now known as the Iron Door and a former grocery store date back to the 1850's.

Second Garrote

This small community has only a dubious hanging tree and an even more doubtful "Bret Harte Cabin" to offer as historical contributions. Supposedly, some 60 men were hanged from the notorious tree, but there is no historical basis for the claim. The cabin's notoriety is the result of a wild supposition that lacks a basis in fact but nevertheless refuses to die.

James P. Chamberlain and James A. Chaffee were young men when they settled in Second Garrote in 1852. There they built a two-story frame house and lived as inseparable friends for the next 51 years. Long before Chaffee died in 1903, their reputation for loyalty to each other and kindness to travelers that passed on Big Oak Flat Road became a legend. Chamberlain lived on for three months after Chaffee's death, but finally took his own life, heatbroken and lonely.

A bit of scholarly speculation by an English professor gave rise to the notion that these two men were models for the protagonists in Bret Harte's story, "Tennessee's Partner." Apparently, from this innocent academic inquiry, the story grew until the house was called "Bret Harte's Cabin" and a 25¢ admission was actually charged.

The house today bears a prominent sign reading "The Bret Harte Cabin," and you will find some who will repeat the story of Chamberlain and Chaffee and tell you positively that Harte developed his story from their lives. Unfortunately, there isn't a scrap of evidence to show that the Gold Country's most celebrated author ever came near the area, much less the "Bret Harte Cabin."

Jacksonville

Jacksonville was a busy town in 1852, but now it's just a small village on the banks of the Tuolumne River where Woods Creek joins it.

The town was named for Colonel Alden Jackson, a

Hanging tree at Second Garrote looks authentic, but it was never used for anything except publicity.

Dressed stone and brick add distinctive touch to old building in Big Oak Flat; iron doors are still intact.

Chinese Camp looks its age; the Catholic Church and graveyard have seen more than a century of service.

Old-time post office in Chinese Camp is still in use. Chinese trees of heaven grow throughout the community.

veteran of the Mexican wars, who discovered gold there in June, 1849. The first orchard in the Southern Mines — called Smart's garden — was planted here; it has only been a few decades since the last apple trees disappeared.

Fire was usually the greatest enemy of the early Gold Rush towns, but flood was responsible for destroying a good part of Jacksonville's original settlement. During the great deluge of 1862, some 80 inches of rain fell on the mountains above Jacksonville within one month, and the resultant high waters got into the second floors of many buildings and washed away most of the weaker structures.

Chinese Camp

One of the most famous and most popular of the southern Gold Rush towns is Chinese Camp, which sits like an oasis amid grass and tarweed fields. There are some good ruins to explore, and one of the wildest fights ever staged in the foothills took place about three miles west of town.

No one really knows just where the Chinese who settled here came from. They may have been employed by English prospectors, or they could have been part of one of the many ship's crews that deserted in San Francisco during the early days of the Gold Rush. At any rate, there were no less than 5,000 Chinese mining the area in the early 1850's.

Trouble came to Chinese Camp in 1856. According to local history, it all started when a huge stone rolled from the diggings of one group to an area where another group was working. A fight developed, and when it ended, the squabbling groups sent out a call for help to their respective tongs — the Sam Yap and the Yan Wo. Each faction felt it had lost face and the only proper thing to do was stage a full scale war between the tongs.

Preparations were hurriedly made, and each side built up an arsenal of crude weapons. Local blacksmiths fashioned spears, tridents, battle axes, pikes, and daggers. A few muskets were brought from San Francisco, and Yankee miners were hired to instruct the combatants in the use of these strange instruments of destruction.

Finally, all was ready. On October 25, 1856, 1,200 members of the Sam Yap fraternity met 900 Yan Wo brothers. Bolstered by speeches and some fire water, the two groups lined up and went after each other, hammer and tongs.

When the smoke cleared, four persons were dead — most likely trampled to death — and another dozen were injured. About 250 were taken prisoner by local

American law authorities. The war was over, stature was regained, and everybody went back to the mines.

Perhaps the most noticeable feature of Chinese Camp today is a profusion of locust-like trees. These are Chinese trees of heaven, planted wherever Chinese settled in the Gold Country. In the shade of the delicate branches, you'll find the post office, Wells Fargo Express Building (in ruins), and an old store. The graveyard is near picturesque St. Francis Xavier Catholic Church on the east side of the highway.

Stent

This quiet village once was a busy camp serving the Jumper, Golden Rule, and other profitable mines. When the gold gave out, so did the settlement. It managed to hang on until the turn of the century, but a fire in 1906 destroyed more than a hundred houses and sealed the town's fate. Today, the only Gold Rush reminder is a neglected old cemetery up by the school-house.

Quartz

All of Quartz's old buildings burned in a 1927 fire, and now there are only a few residential buildings to mark the site of the very productive App Mine. John App, who started the mining in 1856, achieved a measure of fame when he married Leanna Donner, one of the six Donner girls orphaned by the Donner Pass tragedy in 1847.

Knights Ferry

Scout and fur trader William Knight founded Knights Ferry north of Sacramento in 1843, then moved south in 1848 to start a similar operation across the Stanislaus River and take advantage of the Gold Rush traffic.

John and Lewis Dent took over the operation in 1849, after Knight was killed in a gunfight, and later built a grist mill and sawmill downstream from the long covered bridge that now crosses the river just above town. When the town was formally established in 1856, there was some effort to call it Dentville, but Knights Ferry was well-established.

The town's greatest fame derives from a visit by U. S. Grant in 1854. Grant was married to Julia Dent, and he lived with his in-laws during his short stay. The original Dent House still stands in the shade of tall locusts about a block from the main section of town.

The covered bridge you see today was not the first one across the river. The original was built in 1854. It

Old cemetery in Stent is the only link with the past when miners dug fortunes from the nearby hills.

Covered bridge at Knights Ferry is a favorite with photographers. Ruins of a grist mill are just beyond.

Head frame and old buildings of Copper Consolidated Mining Company dominate the scenery in Copperopolis.

Stately brick structure in Copperopolis was originally a church, then became a lodge hall and community center.

was washed away in the floods of 1862, and the present bridge went up soon after in the same place — but eight feet higher. The grist mill that now stands in ruins also is a replacement for the original that was swept down the river along with the bridge.

Two of the most conspicuous Gold Rush buildings that are still standing are the iron jailhouse and the Masonic Hall.

Copperopolis

As its name implies, Copperopolis was one of the few towns in this area that was founded on some mineral other than gold. It was once the principal copper-producing center of California, and boasted a population of 2,000 in 1868 when it was producing ore at a record clip.

Strangely enough, the ore was not smelted anywhere near the mine during the early days. It was carried by cart to Stockton, then by river boat to San Francisco Bay, and finally by sailing ship around Cape Horn to Wales for processing.

Some of the old buildings in town were built in the 1860's of brick hauled from Columbia, where perfectly good stores were being torn down by miners to get at the gold-rich soil under the foundations.

At the south end of town are three notable structures. The biggest — a brick building with huge iron shutters and doors — was once the Federal Armory and served as headquarters for the Copperopolis Blues during the Civil War. Next door are the old warehouse and office buildings of the Copper Consolidated Mining Company. The head frames and tailing piles of the mining operations can be seen across the street.

At the other end of town is the I.O.O.F. Hall, originally a church and lately a community center.

West of Copperopolis, you will see a long stretch of stone fence along Highway 4. While there are some vague stories that name Chinese or Chileans as the builders of this fence, the most logical contender for the honors is James Sykes, a resident of now-vanished Telegraph City.

South of Copperopolis, you cross the Stanislaus River on a bridge that is near the site of O'Byrnes Ferry, a famous crossing point that was used by travelers for more than a century.

Altaville

This junction of State Routes 4 and 49 was first known as Forks in the Road, then Winterton, Cherokee Flat, and finally Altaville. It was settled in 1852 and was a

Miles of stone fence can be seen along Highway 4 in the oak-studded foothills west of Copperopolis.

Prince and Garibardi Store is Altaville's most elegant Gold Rush building. It was built of dressed stone in 1857.

lively little burg during a short period while the placer mining held out.

There are a few buildings worth noting. First is the handsome old Prince and Garibardi Store, a well-preserved, two-story stone building erected more than a century ago. Close by is the oldest iron foundry in California, originally established in 1854 to repair mining machinery and manufacture simple tools.

One of the oldest schools in California can be found on the grounds of the State Highway Maintenance Station near Altaville. The brick building was erected in 1858 and served the community until 1950.

Altaville's name will probably be remembered because it was the starting place of what is today considered by many as the Gold Country's greatest hoax. It was from deep in a mine in nearby Bald Mountain that a human skull — soon to be known to the world as the Pliocene Skull — was taken in 1866 and presented to the scientific world as the remains of a prehistoric man. The argument over authenticity of the skull continued for almost half a century, but it was finally decided that the famous skull actually was Indian in origin and had been placed at the bottom of the mine shaft as an ambitious — and successful — practical joke.

Bret Harte's poem "To the Pliocene Skull," which captures the ridiculous aspects of the whole affair, sug-

This neatly-formed stone corral is one of two visible from the highway between Altaville and Copperopolis.

"Hanging out the wash" is part of the Calaveras County Fair in Angels Camp; at right is a monument to the frog.

Mark Twain deserves special recognition in Angels Camp. His statue is in the city park along main highway.

It won't move now, but this little car and others like it carried tons of ore from Carson Hill mines.

gests the horse laughter that must have filled many a miner's cabin. True to the massive scale in which the joke was conceived, no one connected with the "crime" ever revealed his part.

Angels Camp

This busy little town takes it name from Henry Angel, a member of the 7th Regiment of New York Volunteers that came west in 1848 and founded a trading post where Angels Creek and Dry Creek come together. The town grew fast during the 1850's, became the "Roaring Camp" of legendary fame, and developed into one of the greatest quartz mining centers in the Mother Lode.

The discovery of the quartz lode came about in a curious way. A miner named Raspberry, for whom Raspberry Lane — still a public way in Angels Camp — was named, was having difficulty with his muzzle-loading rifle one day. The ramrod had jammed and in a moment of exasperation he fired the rifle into the ground. The ramrod shot out and struck the ground with force. When he went to retrieve the rod, he found a piece of rock which had broken from the impact and glittered with what was unmistakably gold. Raspberry took almost $10,000 from the new claim in three days and went on to make a fortune following the vein.

Among the most notable buildings still to be seen in Angels Camp are the Angels Hotel, where Mark Twain first heard about the jumping frogs (see page 20), and the imposing jailhouse behind it. At the other end of town is the iron-shuttered, green-and-white Peirano Building. The Angels Quartz Mine, one of the best in the area, was located across from the Catholic Church.

The museum near the north end of town has good collections of minerals and early-day artifacts. In the yard outside are an old traction engine, a cannon, and a section of the world's largest drill core.

True to its legends, the city has erected a monument to the frog along the main street and has placed an imposing statue of Mark Twain in the shady park along Highway 49.

Carson Hill

In its heydey, Carson Hill was considered the richest of all the Mother Lode camps. This was the "classic" ground of the Southern Mines, and many big nuggets were taken from here, including one that was 15 inches

---

FROGS AND FIREWORKS AND FIRE ENGINES

As might be expected, the Gold Rush Country has more than its share of special events. There are county fairs, rodeos, historical celebrations, old-fashioned homecoming parties and town barbecues, and a better-than-average run of art shows, parades, and gem and mineral shows. Some of these events are very similar to those in Los Angeles and San Mateo counties; but a few manage to capture the character of the Gold Rush and thereby offer a special treat for visitors.

Certainly the biggest and noisiest of these events is the Calaveras County Fair held late in May. What really gets the town of Angels Camp jumping during this fair are long-legged frogs. Way back in 1928, the city fathers decided to celebrate the paving of the streets in Angels Camp by staging a frog jump, in honor of Mark Twain's famous story (see page 20). The idea was a great one, and the international frog jumping contest at the County Fair has achieved worldwide recognition.

The fair, itself, has all the trappings of most other county fairs. But the frogs give it a special quality. They arrive by the thousands — some contestants bring them from distant and secret points, and others catch them in the marshy land on the fairgrounds. Any frog at least four inches in length from nose to base of tail is eligible to jump, and fame and riches go to the contestant whose frog jumps the farthest in three consecutive jumps. The strange and mystic rites performed by contestants to encourage their entries into Herculean efforts often overshadow the actual performance by the frogs, and the erratic efforts of man and beast add up to a very entertaining show.

Columbia State Park has more special events than any other spot in the Gold Rush Country, and many a summer weekend is enlivened by a parade or celebration of some sort. One of the most colorful events is the Firemen's Muster held in the spring. Well-drilled fire fighting companies compete against each other, using only antique equipment. Muscle and coordination rule the day, and the high-spirited competition always attracts a big crowd.

A few of the pumpers are on exhibit again at the Fourth of July celebration in Columbia, which also features a barbecue and square dance, plus special events

Frogs get center stage at the Calaveras County Fair.

for the children. Other Fourth of July celebrations are held at Georgetown and Grass Valley-Nevada City. The latter program includes a rodeo and barbecue, walking tours of historical sites, a parade, outdoor art show, gold panning contest, and the traditional fireworks.

The discovery of gold at Coloma is celebrated every January on the weekend closest to the 24th. A parade down the main street of Coloma highlights the Sunday festivities, and there is a Saturday night dance and other special activities.

One noteworthy event just on the fringe of the Gold Rush Country is Bomb Days in Marysville. The Chinese community, which got its start when Marysville was a supply and transportation center for the Northern Mines, pays its respects to Bok Dai, God of Rivers and Streams, every March. Gongs sound the beginning and end of the day of celebration, papier-maché lions and dragons are seen on the streets, and the sound of explosives adds to the excitement. The center of activity is the Bok Dai Temple on D Street near the Yuba River.

Fast-moving motorists often pass up the old Romaggi home, once the showpiece of now-forgotten Albany Flat.

Large plaza in Springfield originally was ringed by buildings. Today, there is only one decaying schoolhouse.

long, 6 inches wide, and 4 inches thick. It weighed 195 pounds and was worth about $43,000 in those days, about $73,000 today. All of the mines in the area produced about $26 million in gold.

The town was named for James Carson, a miner who traveled to the region with George Angel (of Angels Camp) and the Murphy brothers, John and Daniel. There are no buildings of any character left, and the most conspicuous reminder of the mining days is the yawning slash of the Morgan Mine in the hill above town. Fifteen miles of tunnel once ran through the hill, and one of the shafts reaches down almost 5,000 feet.

Along the highway between Angels Camp and Carson Hill sits a large, lonely stone house that is slowly but steadily falling to pieces. This is the Romaggi home, the only remnant of the town of Albany Flat. James Romaggi arrived from Genoa in 1850; scorning gold, he built this house and planted vineyards and orchards to establish one of the finest ranches in the Mother Lode. The stretch of road on either side of the famous house was lined with buildings. But his luck ran out, a drought killed the vines and trees, and Albany Flat faded from sight. Only this curiously complicated building has managed to survive in the parched surroundings.

Jackass Hill

Jackass Hill was in the midst of a very productive placer mining area, and got its name from the braying of the hundreds of mules that were tied up overnight when the pack trains stopped to rest.

Main attraction now is a reconstruction of a cabin where Mark Twain lived for five months as the guests of the Gillis Brothers, who reportedly were hiding in the hills because one had belted a San Francisco bartender with a bottle. While here, Twain wrote about the jumping frog that he heard about in Angels Camp (see page 20). The cabin's site is authentic, but nothing of the actual building is original.

Tuttletown

Tuttletown isn't much more than a wide spot in today's highway, but it prospered during the early days of the Gold Rush. You can still see the ruins of Swerer's store, where Bret Harte was a clerk and Mark Twain was a customer.

The town was named after Judge Anson A. H. Tuttle, who built the first permanent house in Tuolumne County in 1841.

Rawhide

If the term "rawhide" conjures up visions in your mind of Wild West towns and tough hombres, the mining settlement of that name will come as a surprise. This is as quiet an inhabited area as you'll find in the entire Mother Lode.

The farms of today give no hint that this was the location of the Rawhide Quartz Mine, certainly one of the greatest in the area and considered by some as one of the greatest in the world. It produced more than $6 million in gold and was open until 1909.

Shaws Flat

In 1849, Mandeville Shaw planted an orchard on the eastern slope of Table Mountain, and the site became known generally as Shaws Flat. The Mississippi House was built in 1850 as combination post office, store, and bar; it still stands today. Nothing remains of another bar that stood across the street except one of the Gold Country's best legends.

It was at this bar, it is said, that an enterprising bartender supplemented his daily wages in a particularly imaginative way. It seems that he would drop on the bar a wee bit of each pinch of dust that he took from the miners' pokes for their drinks. Now this took slight imagination, but the ingenious part of the larceny lay in his method of recovery.

Periodically leaving the bar to tramp around in the mud made by a little spring behind the building, he would return to his station and carefully pick up with his muddy boots all the gold dust he had dropped and carefully brushed to the floor. Then at night he panned out the mud scraped from his boots — and rich diggings they were. According to the story, he averaged about $30 a night during the week, and several times that on the weekends.

Shaws Flat was the starting place in the career of James Fair who went on to amass a fortune in the Comstock Lode, and there are some who say that it was he who tended bar at that now-vanished saloon across from Mississippi House.

Another remnant of the mining period is the old miner's bell (now on display at the school house) that once was used to call the men to the mines and meetings.

Springfield

Springfield, named for a prodigious spring that gushes forth from between limestone boulders as the source of Mormon Creek, was one of the best laid out of the mining camps. There was a central plaza, and the town spread out over a square mile.

The only building left on the square is the old brick Methodist Church that also served as school and courthouse, and was even converted to military use at the beginning of the Civil War.

Near the intersection of Springfield-Shaws Flat Road and Highway 49 is the site of a lime kiln where limestone was ground into the powder necessary for mortar in brick and stone buildings.

TWO CHANCES TO GO UNDERGROUND

Visitors to the Gold Country have two opportunities to get underground in limestone caves that have been developed commercially.

Mercer Caves (one mile north of Murphys) was discovered by Walter Mercer, a miner, in 1885. Looking for water on a hot September day, he sat down in the shade of a California laurel. A force of cold air on his legs led him to the cave entrance, which he excavated and opened to the public in 1887.

A guide now takes groups on 30-minute tours through an 800-foot series of galleries, entering at the fissure discovered by Mercer and coming out at an artificial opening farther downhill. The temperature is a constant 55° inside the cool, damp caverns. The limestone has taken such shapes as angels' wings and sea anemones, all formed by slow seepage of water over the years.

Since there are steep stairs to climb and low ceilings in some places, toddlers and babes-in-arms are not admitted. Mercer Caves are open from 9 A.M. to 5 P.M. daily in summer and on weekends and holidays in winter.

Moaning Cave is two miles south of Vallecito and about five miles from Mercer Caves. Miners also discovered this limestone cavern, in 1851, and some were brave enough to be lowered part way into it with nothing more than a rope for support and a lantern for illumination.

To visit Moaning Cave, you descend 65 feet on wooden stairs, then 100 feet down a spiral steel staircase. The spiral staircase, added in 1922, unfortunately spoiled the acoustics, and Moaning Cave no longer moans.

Various Indian relics are on display, and an Indian's skeleton lies deep inside the cave. There are several strange rock formations with picturesque names.

Moaning Cave is open from 10 A.M. to 5 P.M. daily in summer and on weekends and holidays in winter.

Columbia is a showcase of Gold Rush architecture. Old brick firehouse is among the numerous restorations.

Columnar Italian cypresses stand before the entrance to St. Anne's Church between Sonora and Columbia.

Columbia

Columbia was — and still is — one of the most important settlements in the Gold Country. When its mines were producing at a record pace in the 1850's, Columbia was called the "Gem of the Southern Mines." It deserves equally high billing today, not for its gold but for its unparalleled collection of reconstructed buildings and mining artifacts.

Every visitor to the Gold Rush Country should visit Columbia. In fact, it makes a good starting point, because here you can pick up a sizable fund of knowledge about architecture and miners' habits that will help you figure out the sometimes-confusing ruins and deserted mining camps located elsewhere.

There is no reason for any first-time visitor to get lost or wonder about the identity of any building. Columbia is maintained as a state park, and everything is clearly labeled. In addition, there is an abundance of maps, guide books, and souvenirs that go to great lengths to explain history and current attractions in detail.

Everything is carefully set out like a multi-course dinner, and gluttony is a far greater threat than starvation. Some visitors will be disappointed at Columbia's blatant commercialism, but there is so much to see and do in this one place that it cannot honestly be avoided.

Historically, Columbia ranked as the largest town in the Southern Mines during its heyday. Some 15,000 people lived here when the earth was giving up a fortune, estimated at $87 million. The town rang with the clamor of hectic activity and the shouts and curses of thousands of miners, gamblers, merchants, dance hall girls, and miscellaneous camp followers who always managed to thrive in the most successful camps. Stagecoaches rattled into town every day, and the roads were crowded with freight wagons bringing in new provisions and merchandise from Stockton.

Gold was discovered here in 1850 by Dr. Thaddeus Hildreth. The camp was first named Hildreth's Diggings, and later American Camp, before finally being christened formally as Columbia at the time of incorporation in 1852. The town was known for its energetic citizens, and many of their efforts have been carefully preserved. Columbia also had a reputation for violence and brutality. In fact, it was here that the Gold Country's most shockingly ugly lynching took place — an event that so deeply affected the conscience of the times that it can be called a turning point in the civilizing process that was to transform the wild camps into mature towns. Briefly, the circumstances were as follows:

A townsman named John Huron Smith weaved into a bar owned by Martha Barclay on one October afternoon and called for a drink. Mr. Smith was in no need of a drink, and in no time an argument broke out between him and Martha, a woman whose personal reputation matched that of her establishment — bad. Her swearing, apparently, caused Smith to push Martha and slap her in rage. Just as he did, Martha's husband, John Barclay, appeared at the door, saw what was happening, and in an instant had drawn his pistol and killed his wife's tormentor.

It might have all been forgotten as a justifiable act, but the Barclays' name was unloved and Smith happened to be a good friend of State Senator J. W. Coffroth, an accomplished orator. Coffroth had no intention of letting the matter die, and he succeeded in warming a mob to lynch heat. They stormed the jail where Barclay was held and, overcoming the guard, took the terrified prisoner down the Gold Springs road to a great flume which towered 40 feet over the crowd. Kangaroo Court was quickly assembled, and it was obvious that only one verdict could be delivered, but before the "jury" returned from their deliberation, the sheriff arrived and attempted to take the prisoner from the mob. The sheriff was swamped by the mob, which then swept Barclay beneath the flume where a hastily-tied noose was put around his neck. The rope was thrown over the flume and the howling mob watched a dozen men jerk the unfortunate man into the air.

But there were no cheers, for there by flickering torchlight they saw in horror their victim hanging onto the rope above his head — in their frantic rush to have justice, no one had thought to tie his hands.

They quickly jerked the rope up and down, but still Barclay held fast — as long as he could keep the rope slack he would live. Then several of the lynchers clambered up the flume supports to shake the rope, but to no avail. Finally, tradition has it, one miner crawled out with a pistol and mercilessly battered Barclay's fists. He dropped, and with a final convulsive kick, died.

The Columbia of today is far removed from that sort of violence, and the emphasis is decidedly in favor of the town's more creative element. More than anything, the town is an architectural showplace for the Mother Lode. Columbia has been burned out a number of times, including a disastrous blaze in 1854, but there are still many original buildings and some excellent reconstructions. St. Anne's Catholic Church, on Kennebec Hill at the west end of town, was finished in 1856 and restored in 1926. The Wells Fargo Express Office, Mills Building, barber shop, Stage Driver's Retreat, Fallon House, and several other buildings from the 1850's are still intact and furnished authentically. The number of restorations increases steadily as more state park funds become available.

Menu at Columbia restaurant gets the attention of hungry visitors. Many buildings are leased to concessionaires.

Authentic stagecoaches (also shown on the cover) are the most popular form of transportation in Columbia.

Beautiful frame building at the north end of Sonora is the St. James Episcopal Church, almost 100 years old.

Sonora's Chinatown is gone, except for one old building off Main Street that was once a dry goods store.

Sonora

In the early 1850's, Sonora and Columbia battled it out for pre-eminence. Today, there is no question about which is the liveliest — Sonora is booming still, and has one of the busiest main streets to be found in the Mother Lode. As seat of Tuolumne County and a trading center for the surrounding cattle and lumber country, Sonora is as bustling as it was a century ago.

Sonora's early history was marred by some ugly incidents between the Mexicans and the Yankees. The town originally was settled early in 1848 by Mexicans, and was known as Sonorian Camp. More Mexicans settled quickly but the Americans weren't far behind, and they did their best to drive off the "furriners" from the south. The vindictive state-wide $20-a-month tax on foreigners was aimed principally at Mexican miners, causing them to band together in defiance. Although there was scattered violence, the Mexicans realized they were beaten and left town in a mass exodus.

Sonora's population dropped from 5,000 to 3,000 practically overnight, and the business community suffered hard times until the tax was repealed in 1851 and Mexicans once again felt safe to return to town.

During its peak production period, Sonora became the Queen of the Southern Mines and one of the wildest towns in the foothills. Washington Street was lined haphazardly with buildings made of adobe, hewn planks, sailcloth, and tin. Horse races and bull-and-bear fights were common, and there was no lack of painted ladies. Liquid refreshment was readily available at any hour of the day or night.

Today, modern façades cover the aged buildings and traffic moves slowly along crowded Washington Street. But even with its modern face, much of Sonora reflects the old days. Just drive a block off the main street and you'll find yourself stepping backward a century. Stewart Street, east of and parallel to Washington, is one of the best routes for this type of leisurely exploration.

Unquestionably, the outstanding piece of old architecture in Sonora is St. James Episcopal Church, which stands at the head of Washington Street on the north end of town. It's not the oldest building in town, but it's the most elegant. Other notable buildings include the I.O.O.F. Hall and the City Hotel.

Sonora was the location of one of the most popular of all Gold Rush Country stories. It concerns the Mexican and his three Indian companions who were found by American miners burning the corpses of two Americans. It took little time once Sonora learned of the act for lynch law to enter the story. But before the proceedings reached the point of no return, the prisoners were rescued just in time by an armed sheriff's posse.

The town was sullen, and rumors spread that a band of guerillas was stationed outside town waiting to sweep in to rescue the prisoners. The sheriff responded to this by rounding up over a hundred Mexicans, most of whom had just arrived in the area, on suspicion of murder. These prisoners were held in a corral to await examination after trial of the Mexican and his Indian friends.

Tension mounted and the town was swollen with hundreds of miners who had come for the trial. Just as court was about to convene, an accidental shot sparked a pandemonious outbreak of gunplay and only by some miracle was bloodshed averted.

The trial began and the miners, whose tempers had been somewhat dampened by the wild outburst of shooting, must have felt even more sheepish — perhaps even ashamed — when the truth about the burning of the bodies was revealed: the Mexican and the three Indians were guilty of nothing more than committing an act of simple charity. They had discovered the murdered bodies of men they had never seen before, and taking time out from their search for gold, had built funeral pyres in accordance with their religious beliefs.

Once the men were freed, the judge turned to examination of the hundred-odd prisoners who had been held in the corral. All were exonerated, and the matter was closed.

Jamestown

Perhaps because of its colloquial name, "Jimtown" is regarded with more affection than many other mining towns. Some of its best wood frame buildings were destroyed in·a tragic fire in November, 1966, but there are still a few wood structures from the 1870's and 1880's, plus some fire-resistant blockhouses dating from the 1850's.

The settlement was founded in 1848 by Colonel George James, a lawyer from San Francisco. James was not known for his scruples, and he was finally forced to leave by disgruntled citizens who objected to all the high-handedness. The town even tried to change its name to American Camp, but "Jimtown" was too firmly fixed to be legislated out of existence.

Vallecito

Vallecito, which means "little valley" in Spanish, sits on the banks of Coyote Creek. It was settled in 1850 by Mexican miners, but did not become a prominent camp until a rich strike in 1852. Still standing at the south

Miner's bell sits atop historical marker in front of the picturesque Union Church in Vallecito.

A disastrous fire in 1966 destroyed many of Jamestown's best buildings. One that survived is the old Emporium.

BEWARE OF THE BITE OF THE BOTTLE BUG

There is a modern-day counterpart to the feverish '49er who rushed around the Gold Country in search of the big strike that would make him rich. But it is not the glitter of gold in the gravel that attracts the eye of these twentieth-century prospectors — it is the glitter of glass. The new craze is for antique bottles.

Old bottles are almost worth their weight in gold. Over the past twenty years, it has become very fashionable to dig, collect, buy, trade, and sell glass containers that once were worth nothing. Otherwise normal citizens will spend back-breaking hours digging through old garbage dumps in search of a whiskey decanter or aspirin bottle that was tossed away long ago by some itinerant miner or busy housewife.

The year 1848 is often called the Gold Rush's Age of Innocence. There was plenty of surface gold and relatively few miners. Everyone got rich and stayed friendly with his equally prosperous neighbors. The equivalent era in bottle collecting was the 1950's. Only a few people were interested in bottles then, and those who had some foresight into the collector's market could go out and dig up bottles by the dozens or even hundreds.

As the prospecting climate changed radically between 1848 and 1849, so it did between the 1950's and the 1960's. As bottles became more popular and more valuable, there was a new rush of miners who wanted a share of the wealth. But the "cream" was gone, and more work was required to get fewer treasures. The commercial diggers worked harder, longer, and smarter than the amateurs, and the best of the diggin's were emptied to benefit newly-opened retail stores.

Today the novice collector is up against tough odds. But as long as there is a ray of hope, there will always be takers. Those who are bitten by the bottle bug can be just as tenacious as the feverish miners of the 1850's.

Beginners in the bottle trade will do well to get familiar with the objects of their search. One of the best collections of antique bottles in the Gold Rush Country can be found in the Mother Lode Bottle and Second Hand Store in Jamestown. Owner Adrian Lyons did his digging during the Age of Innocence, and he has a storehouse that is unmatched in half a dozen counties. Prospectors can check prices and get the latest word on market trends.

Collectors such as Adrian Lyons divide old bottles into seven categories: Bitters, whiskey, poison, soda, beer, ink, and pharmacy. In general, there are more pharmacy bottles buried in the ground than all the other categories combined. In the Mother Lode, the two most commonly found empties carry the labels of Lash's Bitters and Dr. J. Hostetter's Stomach Bitters. Almost every old bottle is worth something, but the most valuable containers are those with distinctive color, writing, or other identification. A 120-year-old plain glass bottle without a mark may be worth less than $10, while a 60-year-old blue cobalt beer bottle may sell for $90 and a 20-year-old Royal Ruby decanter may bring $40.

The exact age of a bottle is difficult to determine. But experts can make a pretty good estimate, based on the

Antique bottles have become valuable treasures.

quality of the glass, the type of seam, and the lip style. For example, a seamed lip reveals that a bottle was machine-made after 1906.

Finding bottles involves a good bit of luck as well as hard work. First you have to find a site. The best burial grounds are the garbage dumps that were used when the old mining towns were enjoying their boom days. Old-time residents often can remember where these dumps were located, but not all of them are willing to tell secrets to strangers. The most ambitious diggers have their best luck by hanging around the local stores or actually knocking on doors in the old residential areas.

Much of the Gold Country is now privately owned, so diggers have to worry about the rights of others. There is also some danger involved. Old mine shafts and caves are notoriously weak, and they may collapse at any time. Always make sure of your footing, and stay out of dark caverns, no matter how promising they may look. You should also be aware of the Federal Antiquities Act of 1906 and the California laws which prohibit excavation by unauthorized persons on certain public lands.

If you're lucky enough to find a garbage dump or old mining camp that has not already been worked and sifted a dozen times, you can get a hundred dollars worth of bottles in a single day. The key to digging for bottles is patience and very careful spadework. Many of the old bottles are very brittle, and a wayward swipe with a shovel can crack or smash the treasure.

Some inexperienced collectors manage to get their bottles home, and then ruin their best specimens while trying to get them clean. Adrian Lyons overcomes this problem with a very simple procedure. He ties a small piece of a kitchen scouring pad on the end of a stiff wire, moistens it with a few drops of water, and carefully swabs out the inside of the bottles. The wire can be bent to reach the corners. Chips and blemishes bring values down considerably, so extreme care is the rule.

There is no doubt that old bottles have a certain fascination. And there are still countless numbers waiting to be dug out of the Gold Rush Country. Beware of the bottle bug — one bite, and you may find yourself waist deep in an old garbage dump, digging madly and mumbling incoherently about that next big strike just over the hill.

Tree-lined streets of Murphys encourage leisurely exploration. Traver Building is one of town's oldest.

Thorpe's Bakery Building, built in the 1850's, has been restored and reopened as an antique shop.

end of town are the Dinkelspiel Store and Wells Fargo Express Office. An old miner's bell and town monument are in front of the Union Church on the main street.

Douglas Flat

Douglas Flat, a serene little community about two miles from Vallecito, has preserved only one stone-and-adobe building from its mining days. The Gilleado Building once served as the town store and bank.

Murphys

Tall locusts line the streets of this grand old town, and in their shade, life goes on much as it has through the decades since the Gold Rush died. In its beautiful setting, Murphys is one of the most charming "live" towns in the Mother Lode, and an ideal place to take a casual stroll and soak up the atmosphere.

Murphys was first settled in July, 1848, by John and Daniel Murphy, and its rich diggings built the substantial town of brick and limestone buildings that you see today.

The most prominent of the old structures is the famous Murphys Hotel, built by Sperry and Perry in 1855 and known for many years as Mitchler's Hotel. You can examine the old register and find names of illustrious travelers in the past — Mark Twain, U. S. Grant, Henry Ward Beecher, Thomas Lipton, J. Pierpont Morgan, Horatio Alger, and many others. You might find the entry "Charles Bolton, Silver Mountain;" no one would have taken this quiet traveler for the notorious highwayman, Black Bart.

Across the street is an old brick-and-limestone building which was used at the beginning as a bakery and miners' supply store. Farther east is another brick-fronted building with the legend "Stephens Bro's. Cheap Cash Store" painted across the side. This was, at an earlier time, Jones' Apothecary Shop.

The I.O.O.F. Hall, Peter Traver Building, Segale Building, and Fish Building, all dating back to the 1850's, are among the other notable old buildings.

St. Patrick's Catholic Church, constructed in 1858, is considered one of the best examples of early construction techniques. Clay used in the bricks was taken from nearby hills.

Famous Jackson tailing wheels at the Argonaut mine are associated with the Gold Rush, but actually are products of the twentieth century. Their electric motors did not whine to a halt until 1934.

THE JACKSON AREA

SHEEPRANCH • MOUNTAIN RANCH • SAN ANDREAS • CALAVERITAS • DOUBLE SPRINGS

VOLCANO • JACKSON • BUTTE CITY • BIG BAR • SUTTER CREEK • AMADOR CITY

JENNY LIND • CAMPO SECO • PALOMA • MOKELUMNE HILL • RAILROAD FLAT

IONE • PLYMOUTH • DRYTOWN • FIDDLETOWN

Sheepranch

This little mountain town is best known as the starting place of the great Hearst fortune. It was here that George Hearst, later United States Senator from California and father of the newspaper tycoon, ran the Sheepranch Quartz Mine. It is said that this mine was a profit-maker from the time the first shovelful was dug.

Mountain Ranch

This was the site of an early sawmill, and there are three or four old Gold Rush buildings that are still in good shape. Most noticeable are the big white Sender's Market (a fine example of Mother Lode architecture), Domenghini's General Store, and the ruins of another hotel and bar on a side street.

Old mining camps in this area range in elevation from Ione (296 feet) to Railroad Flat (2,750 feet). Many back country towns still have a pastoral charm, are seldom bothered by tourists.

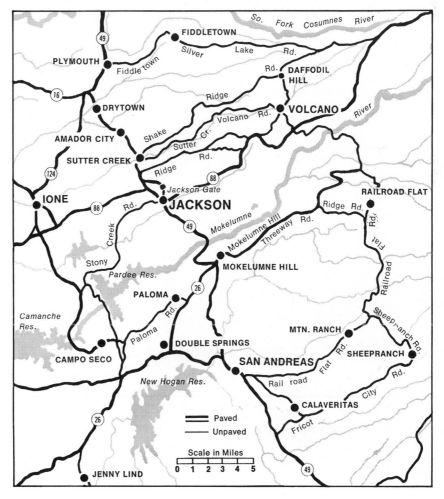

San Andreas

New highway alignments and other demands of modern civilization have stripped San Andreas of most of its mining camp character and left only a few of the original Gold Rush buildings. The remaining examples of early architecture include a dressed stone building that now houses the county library, a two-story I.O.O.F. Hall, and the courthouse which is now home of the Chamber of Commerce and a museum.

The Agostino Building, made of brick and adobe, is located on Court Street near St. Charles. Just west of town is the historic Pioneer Cemetery.

A huge cement plant south of town employs many San Andreas residents today. A century ago, the rich gravels yielded gold to the Mexican miners who settled

"WILL YOU PLEASE THROW DOWN YOUR TREASURE BOX, SIR?"

Black Bart arrived in California almost two decades after the '49ers, but he was such a fascinating old rascal that it's hard to leave him out of any Gold Rush history.

Black Bart was, without doubt, the most famous of all stagecoach robbers — and with good reason. He was credited with 28 robberies between 1877 and 1883, and stage drivers throughout northern California lived in dread of the day when Bart would step out of the brush in some secluded ravine and call out politely, "Will you please throw down your treasure box, sir?"

Bart's character and habits were just as interesting as his success. His working clothes were unique. He dressed in a long linen duster and wore a flour sack over his head with holes cut out for the eyes. He was always on foot and carried only a shotgun and a blanket roll in which was tucked an old axe that he used to break open the strongboxes. Bart chose his locations carefully, and always waited for the stagecoaches at sharp bends in the road where the horses would be moving at a walk.

Bart was gentle with his victims, and never harmed driver or passengers. It was revealed later that he never owned a single shell for his shotgun and could not have fired it even in self-defense. Bart earned the reputation as a poet by leaving bits of doggerel at the scenes of two early robberies. He signed the poetry as "Black Bart, the PO8 (po-ate)."

This colorful career came to an end when Bart was wounded while escaping from a holdup near Copperopolis, and accidentally dropped a handkerchief with the laundry mark "FX07". The mark was traced to a customer of a San Francisco laundry, and police made one of the most surprising arrests in the city's history. Black Bart, the highwayman, turned out to be Charles E. Bolton, one of San Francisco's leading citizens and a man with close connections in the police department.

After his arrest, Bolton confessed to the crimes of Black Bart and told a strange tale of his life as a westernized Jekyll and Hyde. He was born in Illinois as Charles E. Boles and grew up as an intelligent, well-educated citizen. After serving in the Civil War, he emigrated to California in search of gold. Unable to find any legally, Boles decided to try his hand at highwaymanship.

He worked for a time clerking in several stage offices and studied shipments and schedules. Then in August, 1877, he transformed himself into Black Bart and made his first holdup, on the Point Arena-Duncan's Mill stage along the Russian River. His prior knowledge of stage lines and drivers made the job easy. So he tried it again, this time on the Quincy-Oroville stage. Again, all went smoothly. With success came prosperity. Boles moved to San Francisco, took the name of Charles Bolton, and quickly built a reputation as a non-smoking, non-drinking, God-fearing man with big business interests in the mines. He was seen frequently in prominent social circles, always nattily dressed and wearing fancy jewelry.

Whenever more cash was needed to support this high life, Boles-Bolton-Bart would put away his derby and cane and pack up his linen duster and shotgun. Off he would go to the foothills, knock over a convenient stage, and return to more champagne and jeweled pinkies.

Black Bart's fascinating life did not end with his arrest. During his trial in San Andreas, the newspapers made him a legend by distorting his exploits, ballooning the size of his ill-gotten gains, and grossly exaggerating his talent at PO-8-try. Amid much publicity, Bart was convicted and sentenced to six years at San Quentin. He served his sentence, with some time off for good behavior, and was released.

For a while, Bart stayed around San Francisco. But early in 1888, he left for the San Joaquin Valley where he quietly disappeared into the dusty heat. The last verified report found him in Visalia and moving.

For a time, there was a rumor that Wells Fargo had pensioned the old man and sent him away after he agreed not to rob any more stages. This, too, is in the realm of legend, and no one will ever know for sure just what finally happened to the honorable Charles E. Boles of Illinois, the most famous stage robber of them all.

Mild mannered Chas. Boles (above), alias Black Bart. A monument to his career is on the Oroville-LaPorte Road.

Often overlooked by Gold Country explorers, Mountain Ranch has a good collection of ruins.

Just a few feet from a busy highway through San Andreas can be found this collection of early buildings.

the town in 1849, then to Americans who crowded them out in 1850, and finally to thousands of Chinese who had the patience to rework the tailings considered useless by others.

Calaveritas

Calaveritas is another of the towns founded by Mexicans in 1849. It had a brief productive period, and most of the settlement was destroyed by fire in 1858. Now it is a quiet country of cattle and small farms, with scarcely a reminder of the more turbulent years.

Double Springs

When Calaveras County was formed in 1850, Double Springs was named county seat, and kept the honor until the following year.

Double Springs lost its official role under interesting circumstances following a contested election between Mokelumne Hill and Jackson to determine which should be named the new seat (Amador County had not yet been formed). With the issue in doubt, a wagon load of determined boys from Jackson arrived in

A few patches of stucco still cling to disintegrating adobe walls of a long-abandoned store in Jenny Lind.

WHITE-WATER BOATING IS MAKING A BIG SPLASH

The rivers of the Gold Rush Country are among the favorite waterways of an active group of kayakers, canoers, and raft riders who enjoy what is commonly called "white-water boating."

The thrill of white-water boating comes from maneuvering a light craft down a river that has enough current, waves, twists, and turns to pose a real challenge to the boater. It can be enjoyed on any river that is deep enough for the boats, but is not too steep or rocky. Several rivers in the California foothills fit these requirements.

Each river is classified according to its difficulty, on an international scale of I (the easiest) to VI (only for experts). In some cases two sections of the same river may fall into different classifications because of changes in grade or water conditions.

Here are the classifications assigned to some popular Gold Rush Country rivers:

North Fork of the Feather River near Belden, Class IV to V. This is the site of the National Slalom and Downriver races. The slalom is primarily a test of boating skill on a marked course. Numbered gates are formed with poles suspended from overhead lines strung across the river. Contestants must navigate some gates while traveling downstream, others while moving upstream, and still others backward. The course is about ¼-mile long; 18 gates is the minimum. The downriver race is on a grueling, 6-mile course with seven big rapids. This portion of the Feather is suitable only for expert white-water boaters. However, the Feather River between Oroville and its junction with the Sacramento River is Class II at the upper end, Class I farther downstream, and quite suitable for beginner and intermediate groups.

Sacramento River between Redding and Red Bluff is Class I-II. This is a popular two-day run for kayaks, canoes, and rafts.

The lower Yuba River from State Route 20 bridge to Daguerra Dam at Brown's Valley is Class I or II — a very nice one-day trip.

Bear River is small, but there is enough water in the spring for some good boating; this is Class I-II. Boats can be put in the water near the State Route 65 bridge near Wheatland and taken out at one of the county roads downstream.

South Fork of the American River is very popular with kayak groups. The Coloma-Lotus area is Class II and III; upstream from Coloma and downstream from Lotus, the river is Class III-IV.

Cosumnes River is small, but good for spring and early summer boating, particularly in the Bridgehouse-Sloughhouse area. Upstream from Bridgehouse, the river is too steep and rocky.

American River near Fair Oaks is Class I and II — an excellent place for beginners. There are several good access points, and more will become available as the lower American is developed as part of the Sacramento County Parkway plan.

Mokelumne River has one very nice boating section (Class II or III) above State Route 49. Boats can be put in at the Electra Powerhouse and taken out at the highway bridge.

Stanislaus River is Class II and III from Parrots Ferry to State Route 49. The river is in a beautiful and isolated canyon above Parrots Ferry, but the rough water is suitable only for experts and commercial rafters.

White-water boating can be enjoyed any time of the year, except when the rivers are flooding or are very low. Since it is impossible to make any sort of a loop trip on the rivers, arrangements must be made in advance to get the boats to the starting points and then take them out at the ends of the runs.

White-water boating is exciting, but not really dangerous as long as boaters understand the special problems created by light boats on fast waters. A few hours of practice on quiet waters is required before a beginner can face a churning current and rocky rapids. Protection from the cold water is usually provided by a wet-suit jacket such as that worn by a skin diver. Life jackets are standard equipment.

Beginners will do well to join one of the organized groups that take frequent trips on the Gold Country rivers. The largest organization is the River Touring Section of the Mother Lode Chapter of the Sierra Club (P. O. Box 1335, Sacramento, California 95806). In addition to arranging several trips a year, this group conducts classes for beginners in paddling techniques, safety, water reading, equipment, and self-rescue. White-water boaters have to expect to tip over once in a while and must be prepared to take care of themselves.

Maneuvering the rapids on the Stanislaus River.

Running the slalom on the Feather River.

First settled by Mexicans, Campo Seco profited more from copper mining than from short-lived gold digging.

On a hill above town, two collapsing stone buildings remain as remnants of Campo Seco's Chinatown.

Double Springs to offer the county clerk there a casual libation. One led to another, so the story goes, and it was an easy matter for the Jackson crew to pack up official paraphernalia and hustle it off to Jackson.

Today Double Springs consists of the mellow old two-story stone home built by Alexander Reid Wheat in 1860 that has housed seven generations of his family. Behind the house stands the original courthouse, which was built of camphor wood shipped from China and at one time housed a courtroom, recorder's office, private living quarters for the county clerk, and even a saloon.

Jenny Lind

This was once the hub of mining activities on the lower Calaveras, but the town has retreated to a point of sleepy idleness. There are only a few old frame houses, an I.O.O.F. Hall resting on old stone foundations, and the ruins of an adobe building.

The name of the town remains something of a minor mystery. There is no evidence that the famous Swedish Nightingale ever came within 2,000 miles of the place.

Campo Seco

Campo Seco is not often included on tours of the Gold Country, but the tiny hamlet has an unusual number of photogenic ruins. One in the center of town is the remainder of the two-story Adams Express Buildings; across the street is the rapidly disintegrating wooden butcher shop. On a small local road northwest of the center of the village are two stone buildings with collapsed wooden roofs, the only remains of the town's Chinese section.

Oddly enough, Campo Seco enjoyed its greatest boom times not from the rich placer diggings of the early Gold Rush days, but from the Penn Copper Mine that opened in the 1860's.

Paloma

Paloma began life as a placer mining camp in 1849 and is presently a small collection of undistinguished frame buildings on a wide place in the road. Behind the local historical marker are the ill-kept remains of an *arrastra* which was once used to crush ore.

A favorite with tourists, Mokelumne Hill gets some of its charm from old cemetery and tall cypress trees.

Oldest three-story building in the Gold Country is the well-constructed IOOF Hall in Mokelumne Hill.

Mokelumne Hill

"Mok Hill" is one of the most popular Mother Lode towns because of its winding streets, good collection of early architecture, and unmistakable mountain flavor.

Many of the buildings in Mokelumne Hill are built of light brown stone known as rhyolite tuff, a material common to much of the Mother Lode. Best-known reminders of the Gold Rush are the Odd Fellows Hall (first three-story building in the Gold Country), the remains of the Meyer Store, and the famous old Léger Hotel with its elegant balconies (see page 80). The beautiful wooden Congregational Church, built in 1856, sits on columns of fitted stone blocks.

The town was started in November, 1848, when hungry miners financed a man named Syrec to start a supply depot for the nearby diggings.

In an area that was ridden by violence and international friction, Mokelumne Hill seems to have had more than its share. For instance, there was a stretch of 17 weeks, tradition has it, when there was at least one murder every weekend; another time five people were killed in a week.

The diggings were rich in the "Mok Hill" region, so rich in fact that in certain areas claims were limited to 16 square feet. But this wealth didn't keep the Americans busy with their own work all the time. Unlike many other camps which had one "foreign war," Mokelumne Hill had two.

South of town, the now-vanished camp of Chili Gulch was the scene of the "Chilean War" in which Hillites conquered the stubborn Dr. Concha in 1849. But this was not before several men were killed. Here, at least, there was some justification, because Dr. Concha was working his claim with peon labor and had registered claims in the names of men who were slaving for him. Slavery was one universally forbidden practice in the Gold Country.

The "French War," which occurred two years later, was a different matter. French miners who, as a group, had had excellent luck in their mining, raised a French flag above their diggings on a rise, appropriately named French Hill, that overlooks the town. The Americans, using the excuse that the French were defying the American Government, swarmed up the hill and drove the French from their claims. As far as anyone knows, the excuse was hollow — and only envy and greed provoked the incident.

Railroad Flat

This little mountain settlement was a placer and quartz mining center for a few years. Far from the nearest railroad, it was named after a few hundred feet of wooden track laid by a miner to carry ore in a mule-pulled car.

Across the road from the historical marker is a grocery store built during the hamlet's early history. In the back part of the building, you can still see the windows and numbered boxes of the first post office in the area (now abandoned).

Volcano

Volcano is unquestionably one of the most important stops in the Gold Country — not only for what it was in the 1850's but for what it is today.

Volcano's earliest residents were a lively bunch, as intent on developing their little city as they were on digging for the loot. Today's residents are also a lively crew, and the community continues to preserve its heritage by stint of hard work and neatness of spirit. Few towns in the Mother Lode have as many things to see, and such a tidy setting to see them in.

Volcano is a misnomer. It is true that the town is situated in a natural cup in the mountains, but there is nothing volcanic about the area's mountain structure. Evidently, the settlers just took one casual look around them and settled for first impressions.

Gold was first discovered here in 1848 by members of the New York 8th Regiment, Mexican War Volunteers. The first mining camp grew quickly into a city of 5,000 people, and was the lively center of a rich mining area that produced some $90 million in gold. When the placer workings gave out, hydraulic mining tore the soil away from the limestone bedrock and sent it funneling through the sluices.

Volcano claims many "firsts" in California's cultural development: first public library, first literary and debating society, first astronomical observatory, first "little theatre" movement. It also had an abundance of saloons and fandango halls to fill the miners' idle hours. At one time, there were three dozen saloons and three breweries. One of the crumbling stone buildings still standing on the west side of the main street housed two separately operated bars.

There are many other remains of the early town —

Picturesque main street of Volcano is lined with old buildings, including lodge hall and remodeled trading post.

You can't miss the balconied, vine-covered St. George Hotel as you enter Volcano from the south.

the old jail, a brewery built in 1856, the Odd Fellows-Masonic Hall, the Adams Express Office, the Lavezzo Building that once served as a wine shop, the old St. George Hotel, and others. All are marked for your convenience.

Perhaps the most unusual reminder of Volcano's past is "Old Abe," the cannon that helped to win the Civil War without ever firing a shot.

Volcano's Union volunteers wheeled out "Old Abe" to put down a threatened Confederate uprising. Control of Volcano might have meant that the area's gold would be diverted to the Southern cause. The story is told that in the absence of iron cannon balls, Union men gathered round, river-smoothed stones. "Old Abe" won the battle without firing a shot — its mere presence squelched the uprising.

Volcano's nearest neighbor of any size is Jackson, and during the 1850's the two towns had a sporting rivalry typical of the times. Once a man from Jackson caused quite a stir in Volcano, so reported a Jackson paper at the time, when he produced a $20 gold piece to pay his hotel bill and buy the house a round of drinks.

TOURING ON TWO WHEELS

The Gold Rush Country is not ideal terrain for bicycling. There are too many deep river canyons and steep mountain slopes to encourage casual family outings on a Sunday afternoon. But this does not mean that the foothills are completely closed to the two-wheelers. With some advance scouting and careful selection of routes, you can make very pleasant one, two, or three-day trips through some of the most scenic mining areas.

Bicycling is a great way to explore any part of the countryside. You get a whole new perspective of the terrain, and you see things that would normally be just a blur through the window of a fast-moving car. In the Sierra foothills, you get a better idea of the natural obstacles that the miner faced on his travels, and you can't help but feel a new kinship for the '49er and his mule when you laboriously push your bike over that last hill and look down into some little mining town.

Advance scouting may take some of the pure adventure out of Gold Country cycling, but it is a necessary evil. Unless you're a road-hardened rider on a 10-speed bike, you'll have trouble enough making a pre-planned route, and an unplanned sojourn down some road that just "looks good" may well wind up with arduous hill climbing or time-consuming backtracks.

Whenever possible, select routes on the back roads. State Route 49 is often crowded with cars and lumber trucks, and cyclists can have a difficult time of it. Don't be afraid to walk your bike. Most bike rides normally involve a few miles of heel-and-toeing anyway, and you'll feel much safer walking at the side of the road in heavy traffic than pedaling uncertainly along the shoulder. It isn't always possible to make complete loop trips on Gold Country roads, so you may have to make advance arrangements to have a car or truck drop you off at the starting point and then show up at the finish.

One of the best single-day runs in the foothills is from Volcano to Sutter Creek. A paved road leads 12 miles through forest and fields on a gentle downhill run that is great for beginners. The creek is beside you all the way — a torrent in spring, and barely more than a quiet trickle in late summer. The road is bumpy in spots and often narrow, but traffic is very light. There are many opportunities for picnicking; tables and fire pits are located at one spot seven miles from Volcano.

Hard-working cyclists on Amador County back road.

Organized bicycle clubs — such as those affiliated with American Youth Hostels, Inc. (AYH) — often schedule more rigorous trips. It is not uncommon for these enthusiastic cyclists to cover 30 to 50 miles a day, including some rigorous walking. One of the most active groups in the Gold Country is the Foothill Swiftwalkers A.Y.H. Club of Sacramento. Typical extended trips for this group are a three-day ride between Truckee and Sacramento (about 100 miles) and a four-day ride from Quincy to Nevada City via state routes 89 and 49 (about 120 miles). Bikes and riders are transported to and from Sacramento in trucks or by train. Cars sometimes accompany the groups to carry camping and cooking equipment, and to take care of emergencies. The cyclists usually stay overnight in campgrounds.

These organized trips can be rugged for inexperienced cyclists, but seasoned group leaders and careful advance preparations can often ease the pain. Clubs like the Swiftwalkers usually will take non-members who want to try one of the trips before committing themselves to a group membership. For more information, contact W. L. Krill, 5305 Fernwood Way, Sacramento, California 95841.

Whether you're traveling in a family group or with one of the organized clubs, plan on carrying most of your own gear. Saddle bags and carriers are available that will hold changes of clothes, personal items, first aid and tool kits, camera, flashlight, maps, and money. The investment is minor, and self-sufficiency will serve to increase the feeling of adventure that comes with cycling in the Gold Country.

Limestone skeleton of Wells Fargo Office is one of several old ruins that give Volcano's main street a ghostly air.

Gaily decorated National Hotel is at the south end of Jackson's narrow, busy main street.

The editor implied that it had been so long since anyone in Volcano had seen a $20 piece that they gathered around the Jacksonian with curiosity and admiration.

It took only a week for the editor in Volcano to straighten Jackson around. It wasn't curiosity or admiration of the gold piece, it seems, it was Volcano's awe that anyone from Jackson should have that much cash in the first place, and further that he would use it to buy someone else a drink and to pay his hotel bill before slipping out of town.

Jackson

Jackson is one of the Mother Lode towns that has kept up with progress and now shows a modern face to visitors. City planners are striving to preserve some of the Gold Rush feeling, but the demands of twentieth-century commerce keep getting in the way.

The town was first named "Bottileas," a label affixed by Chilean miners who were impressed by the abundance of bottles dropped at the spring that served as a watering spot for passing miners.

One of the most interesting buildings in town is the old Brown House, built in the 1860's on a hill about two blocks east of the main part of town. It now serves as the county museum. You'll also find the I.O.O.F.

St. Sava's Serbian Orthodox Church, first to be built in U. S., is one of Jackson's most interesting buildings.

Quiet side streets of Sutter Creek have a number of quaint nineteenth-century buildings that are still in use.

Hall and the restored National Hotel (Louisiana House) on the narrow little main street. St. Sava's Serbian Orthodox Church, built in 1893, is unusual for its architectural style.

The two most important factors in Jackson's economy for many decades were the Argonaut and Jackson mines north of town. The Argonaut, easily recognizable today by its lofty water tank, was opened in 1850 and operated continuously between 1893 and 1942. The Kennedy Mine started in 1856 and operated sporadically until 1942. Its most famous features are the huge tailing wheels built in 1912 to carry waste gravels away from the mine. They can be seen from Highway 49, or you can walk up for a closer view by driving out the Jackson Gate Road and taking the well-marked trails. There are two wheels on each side of the road. Three are standing in their original positions, and the fourth lies in ruins — the victim of a violent wind storm.

Butte City

Butte City enjoyed a boisterous but very short life in the 1850's. Once a rival for Jackson, it practically disappeared when the gold gave out. Today, there is only the badly weathered Ginocchio Store, built in 1856. A sturdy fence protects it from vandals.

Big Bar

Big Bar was the most important camp on the Mokelumne River in the 1850's, when a busy ferry moved miners, gold, and supplies along the Gold Rush Highway. When nearby placers gave out, the center of activity moved to Mokelumne Hill.

Sutter Creek

Sutter Creek (or "Crick" as it is often called) is named for John Sutter, who camped here in 1848 with a group of Indians. The town actually got started when a few of the early miners erected a community tent to use on rainy Sundays when they couldn't get to Jackson or Drytown. It later achieved permanency as an important supply center for the quartz mines that started up in the 1850's.

The town's main street is lined with old buildings, many with balconies. Among the oldest structures are the Masonic and I.O.O.F. Halls (1865), Methodist Church (1862), Malatesta Building (1860), stone Brignole Building (1859), and Bellotti Inn (1860).

One of Sutter Creek's most famous success stories concerns Leland Stanford. As a young man, Stanford acquired some means as a merchant in Sacramento, and picked up a stake in Sutter Creek's Lincoln Mine as payment of a merchant's debt. He worked the claim but suffered repeated failures. Discouraged, Stanford decided to sell the property for $5,000, but was talked out of it at the last minute by Robert Downs, the mine foreman. Not long afterward, a big strike was made and the Lincoln Mine became a bonanza. With this wealth as a start, Stanford joined Hopkins, Crocker, and Huntington to build the Central Pacific Railroad and went on to become a U.S. Senator, Governor of California, and founder of Stanford University.

Amador City

A miner from San Jose named Jose Maria Amador gave his name to this little town and the county that was separated from Calaveras County in 1854. Quartz provided the economic base for Amador City, and the head frame of the very rich Keystone Mine can be seen on the eastern slope above the south end of town. The Mine House (see page 81) is located in the original Keystone Consolidated Mining Company brick buildings.

Highway 49 passes through the middle of Amador

City, and you'll have no trouble locating the deserted Imperial Hotel, the restored Amador Hotel, and the local museum.

Ione

This little town has been part of the Gold Country since the earliest days of the Gold Rush, not as a mining camp, but as a stage stop, agricultural center, clay and sand producer, and rail center.

Like so many other towns that started as temporary camps, Ione's dignified name (she was the heroine of *The Last Days of Pompeii*) was chosen only after the townsfolk grew embarrassed about "Freezeout" which had been preceded by "Bedbug." The first two may have been accurate, but they did little for civic pride.

Plymouth

During the 1850's, the settlements of Plymouth and Pokerville grew up side by side on a dry flat. Plymouth has managed to survive as an agricultural center, but Pokerville has vanished except for one old brick-and-stone building.

There is very little in Plymouth to remind you of the Gold Rush. The most notable building is the old mining company's brick office building on the main street between the bank and the old Roos Building.

Drytown

Founded in 1848, Drytown is the oldest town in Amador County. From its name, you might guess that it had been settled by men of abstemious habit. But the town actually supported 26 saloons in its prime, and temperance was not a widespread virtue. Dry Creek was the source of the title.

The placer diggings gave out in 1857, and a fire soon leveled the old town. Now there is only one brick building, dating from 1851, standing on the east side of the highway. A converted dance hall is the home of a little theater group.

Fiddletown

This sleepy, tree-shaded village lies in the center of a prosperous dry farming belt that is still worked in many cases by descendants of the pioneers who settled here in the 1850's.

The flavor of the early days is preserved by several old structures including a couple of stone buildings, a rammed earth adobe that supposedly was built as a

Rusting head frame of the once-rich Keystone Mine overlooks old buildings on highway through Amador City.

Now deserted, Amador City's Imperial Hotel was once an important stopping point on Gold Country highway.

The original Stewart Co. store (brick building on the right) was built during Ione's boom times in the 1850's.

Chinese built this rammed earth adobe in Fiddletown; examples of this construction technique are rare.

Informal tourist center of Fiddletown is the solid-looking Schallhorne Blacksmith and Wagon Shop.

Chinese joss house, and the Schallhorne Blacksmith and Wagon Shop built in 1870.

Fiddletown's fame must, in part, rest on its name. Founded by Missourians in 1849, it was named by an elder in the group who described the younger men as "always fiddling." It kept the name for almost 30 years, but in 1878 the name was changed to Oleta by the state legislature. This was done at the insistence of Judge Purinton, so the story goes, who had become known in Sacramento and San Francisco, much to his embarrassment, as the "Man from Fiddletown." The old name, whose charm was quickly recognized by Bret Harte and immortalized by him in "An Episode in Fiddletown," was restored in the 1920's.

It was here that a certain Judge Yates reached the limit of his patience in listening to an outlandish whopper and created a classic in courtroom procedure. He heard all he could stand before he finally turned to the witness, banged down his gavel, and said, "I declare court adjourned. This man is a damned liar. Court in session."

Eight miles northeast of Plymouth on Aukum Road is the D'Agostini Winery built in 1856 by Adam Uhlinger. The original wine cellar is still in use.

TRYING YOUR LUCK WITH A GOLD PAN

One good way to catch some of the spirit of the colorful Gold Rush days is to try your luck with a gold pan along one of the historic gold streams. Youngsters especially will find a short session with the gold pan exciting.

Most gold streams were very efficiently gleaned by the early miners, but you may still find gold flakes and small nuggets washed down during spring floods or lost during earlier mining operations. The California Division of Mines and Geology estimates that a prospector willing to toil long hours can still recover from 50 cents to $1 a day in gold.

Previous mining activity is one of the best indications of the presence of gold. Look in old mine tailings. Generally, the ground at the tail of an old sluice is a good place to try.

A stream deposits gold-enriched gravel where the current slows — where the grade decreases — where the channel widens, deepens, turns, or joins another stream. Likely places for panning are at the upstream end of gravel bars, and the downstream side of boulders.

Since gold tends to settle at the bottom of coarse materials, a shallow gravel bar is easier to work than a deep one — look for bedrock ridges in the water or on the immediate banks. Gold often settles in pockets of gravel in bedrock. Many prospectors use a long-handled spoon or knife to get into crevices.

Other materials collect in the same sort of place that gold does. Often the amateur mistakenly collects pyrite ("fool's gold") or one of the bronze-colored micas. In comparison with real gold, fool's gold is usually found in its crystalline form (small cubes), has a brassy luster on freshly broken surfaces, and will fracture rather than crush as gold will. Mica is light, settles slowly in water (in contrast to the way gold drops), and scales into flakes.

Gold has a color of its own. It has a luster in sun or shade, cuts easily with a knife, and never scales or fractures. You can mistake fool's gold for real gold many times — until you've seen real gold in your pan.

For an excellent primer on panning for gold, write the California Division of Mines and Geology, Ferry Building, San Francisco, 94111, and ask for the free pamphlet titled *Basic Placer Mining*.

Gold panners first fill the pan with gravel and mud.

Large pieces of gravel are removed by hand.

Nugget this size is a rare find today.

Rocking motion gets rid of gravel, coarse sand.

Small stone buildings originally used by Chinese are part of Marshall Gold Discovery State Park in Coloma. Nearby is a large museum with good displays and a collection of early mining equipment.

THE PLACERVILLE AREA

EL DORADO • DIAMOND SPRINGS • PLACERVILLE • SHINGLE SPRINGS • COLOMA
LOTUS • PILOT HILL • GREENWOOD • GEORGETOWN
GARDEN VALLEY • KELSEY • VOLCANOVILLE

El Dorado

Only a few stone relics of the Gold Rush days remain in this faded little community, known as Mud Springs when it was the center of rich placer diggings. Actually, the town was a stop on the Carson Emigrant Trail before 1848, but it was not named and incorporated until the miners arrived in 1849 and 1850.

Diamond Springs

This was another stop on the Carson Trail that mushroomed with the Gold Rush. It was one of the richest spots in the Placerville area, and the population once hit 1,500. But now, with the gold gone and the traffic rerouted, Diamond Springs just sits there in the sun without causing much of a stir.

You'll find the I.O.O.F. Hall—a grand old frame building built in 1852 on a foundation of brick and dressed stone—on a hill north of the main street, and one or two other relics that are slowly crumbling away.

Placerville

One of the first camps settled in 1848 by miners who branched out from Coloma was Dry Diggin's, so called because of the scarcity of water to wash the gold-laden soils. Three prospectors—Daylor, Sheldon, and Mc-Coon—made the first strike and took $17,000 in gold in one week.

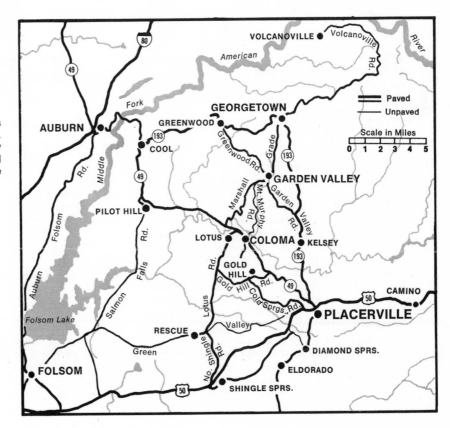

The Gold Rush's first mining camps are found on both sides of Coloma. Georgetown-Garden Valley-Kelsey Road offers spectacular views. Road to Volcanoville is unpaved for the last nine miles.

The news spread quickly, and Dry Diggin's rapidly became one of the most prosperous camps in the Mother Lode and one of the most important towns in the Sierra Nevada. Its name was changed to Hangtown in 1849 after a series of grisly lynchings, and finally to Placerville in 1854 to satisfy self-conscious pride.

Hangtown certainly was not a misnomer. There are several on record, the first of which was actually a triple hanging. Two Mexicans and a white man were accused of robbing a Frenchman named Caillous of 50 ounces of gold dust and were strung up after only a single night's deliberation. "Irish Dick" Crone was another who felt the hangman's noose after he knifed a man to death over a turn of the cards in a game of monte. Two Frenchmen and a Chilean were set swinging for a crime that no one can seem to remember.

But despite this, Hangtown was quick to establish itself as a key point in California history, and one of the most populous of the early mining centers. Even when the gold supply began to diminish, the town remained an important stop on the route between the Northern and Southern mines, a station on the routes of the Pony Express and Overland Mail, and a supply center for other mining camps. Its greatest period of

NEITHER SNOW NOR RAIN...NOR GLOOM OF NIGHT

Placerville had a valid reputation as a busy commercial center during the nineteenth century, and its most notable citizens did very well financially. But the hearts of its citizens belong to a man who made very little money while establishing a new level of pioneer spirit. He was John A. "Snowshoe" Thompson, a truly dedicated mailman who lived by his creed and never allowed snow, nor rain, nor gloom of night to stay him from the swift completion of his appointed rounds.

Strangely enough, Snowshoe Thompson never wore a pair of snowshoes in his life. He was a skier, and he spent 12 long winters skiing across the Sierra to deliver the mail between Placerville and Carson Valley, Nevada, at a time when no other man would do the job.

Thompson was a native of Norway who came to America with his parents to farm in the Midwest. He was attracted by the lure of California gold, and at the age of 24, he set out to make his fortune. A few years of mining around Placerville produced little more than a tired back, so Thompson returned to farm life in 1854 to earn his bread and beans.

But he never lost his love of the mountains. When he heard that the U. S. Post Office was having trouble getting carriers for the Sierra Nevada crossing, Thompson decided that opportunity was knocking at his door. He gave up ranch life, made himself a pair of skis, and applied for the job at the Placerville post office.

Thompson's skis were not very good, according to modern standards. They were handhewn from green oak, stood about 10 feet tall and must have weighed 25 pounds. But they got him over the snow, even when he was weighted down with 80 pounds of mail. To reduce his own load, Thompson did not carry blankets or firearms and restricted his food supply to a pocketful of salt pork and biscuits. The 90-mile trip from Placerville to Carson Valley took three days, and the trip back another two.

Snowshoe Thompson did his job diligently for 12 years. Apparently, he never got seriously ill or was ever injured, and the mail went through regularly. The mailman also became a personal messenger, delivering news and reports of mountain conditions and snow depths. He became famous for his rescue of James Sisson, a miner

Snowshoe Thompson at work in the Sierra.

who was stranded in a mountain cabin in Lake Valley. Sisson was half-frozen and half dead from hunger when Thompson found him. After providing the miner with fire and food, Snowshoe went to get help in Placerville. Five volunteers made a sled and towed Sisson into Carson Valley. But Thompson wasn't through. When a doctor decided that Sisson's legs had to be amputated, the durable Norwegian crossed the summit yet again to bring chloroform from Placerville and ease the patient's pain.

Snowshoe Thompson lost his job when the trans-Sierra railroad was completed. His total income as a mailman was miniscule because of bad contracts and lack of government funds. Even after his retirement, Thompson was refused any pension or retroactive payment, and he died a poor man in 1876.

It is sad that so brave a man could not be properly rewarded. As one of the Gold Country's most inspiring heroes, Snowshoe Thompson deserved some comforts to go along with his everlasting fame.

Stone and brick building on Placerville's main street managed to survive the devastating fire of 1856.

Old City Hall and Justice Court have been occupied since Placerville's heyday as the largest of the mining camps.

stable growth actually came after the California Gold Rush was over. When the Comstock Lode was discovered in Nevada, the Placerville Road became the main route across the mountains for miners eager to abandon the fading gold for the promise of silver.

Although most of old Placerville has been modernized, the street pattern is still based on the trails marked off by the miners' pack mules. And if you look at the stores from the rear, away from the glitter of new façades, you can feel the town's age.

There are some old buildings left in the main business district. The Pony Express Building at 10 Sacramento Street, just off Main Street, originally was a harness shop when first built in 1858. A Pony Express historical marker can be found in the alley behind the building. The Old City Hall was built in 1857, and the building next door was built in 1862 from funds accumulated by Immigrant Jane Stuart who drove a herd of horses across the plains and then sold them. A rock building on the south side of Main Street dates from 1852 and was one of the few structures to withstand the great fire of 1856 that destroyed almost all of the old Hangtown. The I.O.O.F. Hall has been in use since 1859.

Sites now occupied by Raffles Hotel and Hangman's Tree were both important in early Placerville history.

"SO MISUNDERSTOOD, SO MISJUDGED...SO ALTOGETHER SLANDERED"

The saddest figure of the California Gold Rush has to be James Wilson Marshall, the man who started it all. Despite the fact that he was the first to discover gold in Coloma, Marshall never made any money from his discovery, and his fame only led to a life of misery.

Marshall had the fortune — or perhaps the misfortune — to be in the right place at the right time. His gold discovery was an accident, pure and simple, and it is evident that if he had not picked up a few flakes of gold in the tailrace of a mill, then someone else would have found it somewhere else within a year or so. There was just too much gold on the surface to be ignored by the California settlers who were gradually pushing up into the foothills.

James Marshall was born in New Jersey in 1810, was given a moderate education for the day, and was taught his father's trade as a millwright. Like many young men of this time, young James started west after fame and fortune. He worked for a time in Illinois and Indiana and then in 1844 joined a wagon train that took him into Oregon's Willamette Valley. After a short stay, he joined a group heading into California, and arrived at Sutter's Fort in July, 1845, about 10 years after leaving New Jersey.

Marshall worked for Sutter until he could save enough money to buy some land and livestock in Butte County. When the Bear Flag War broke out in the summer of 1846, he joined the American settlers and fought until the end of the year. By the time he returned to his ranch, the stock were scattered and lost. He had no choice but to sell the ranch and rejoin Sutter.

In August, 1847, Sutter and Marshall agreed to build a sawmill in the foothills, with Sutter to provide the men and money and Marshall the leadership. It was when this mill was almost completed that Marshall found gold in the tailrace. It was January 24, 1848, and James Marshall skyrocketed to world prominence at the age of 37 years, 3 months, and 16 days.

During 1848, Marshall and Sutter tried to claim ownership of the Coloma property and charge a commission for any gold found by other miners. Only a few of the most gullible newcomers paid any money to Marshall or honored his self-imposed property rights, and he was forced to sell one-third of his timber and mill rights at the end of the year to raise money. Even though it did him no good, Marshall continued to haggle with the miners and got them so riled up that they finally attacked the millhands and drove Marshall off the land.

It was at this point that Marshall seriously undermined his own future. He began to claim supernatural powers that enabled him to pinpoint the richest gold deposits. When he refused to divulge the location of any of these rich diggin's, the miners grew very resentful and even threatened to lynch Marshall if he didn't lead them to the treasure.

Marshall fled for his life and tried to start over as just another miner. But his face was too well known, and greedy miners dogged his steps wherever he went in the

Stilted portrait of an embittered hero.

vain hope that a new bonanza would be uncovered on Marshall's next claim.

This constant harassment turned Marshall into a bitter man. He felt that the world — or at least the state — owed him something for his sensational discovery, and he interpreted every setback as a conscious effort by somebody to cheat him out of his divine rights. He became a recluse, and his eccentric behavior turned away all but a few close friends.

In 1872, the state of California appropriated the discoverer of gold a $200-a-month pension. Marshall moved to Kelsey and built a blacksmith shop. He worked there and lived in the Union Hotel until his death in August, 1885, at the age of 73. The state pension was cut in half after 1874 and eliminated entirely in 1876. During his last years, Marshall was forced to live off handyman jobs, handouts, and the few pennies he could pick up by selling his autograph.

Margaret A. Kelley, a friend of Marshall's during his embittered old age, once wrote that "probably no man ever went to his grave so misunderstood, so misjudged, so misrepresented, so altogether slandered as James W. Marshall." This may be true. But it is also true that Marshall made the worst of his fate, and instead of building on his good fortune, he misplayed it into the instrument of his destruction.

Some historians go so far as to claim that Marshall got exactly what he deserved, and that he would have been a miserable old man even if he had never been cursed as the discoverer of gold. At the same time, this strange man engenders real pity. He wandered into history quite by accident and then was buffeted and bruised for the rest of his days just because he lacked the cunning to take advantage of a lucky situation. It is better to avoid judgments in hindsight, and instead acknowledge the man's place in history and let him rest in peace.

Stone shell of Wells Fargo Building in Shingle Springs looks out of place next to the busy modern highway.

Discoverer of gold is buried beneath his monument in Coloma. Statue's hand points to discovery site.

You can visit Big Cut, one of the area's richest ore deposits, by following Big Cut Road southeast of town. At the top of the hill, you can see how the hydraulic nozzles cut away the cliffs. A million dollars in gold reputedly was taken from a single acre of this rich hill. Mining continued until 1900.

Shingle Springs

Shingle Springs is much more intent on serving the modern motorist than preserving an air of antiquity, but you'll still find a well-preserved, two-story Wells Fargo Express building on the south side of the highway.

The town was named for the cool spring that flowed near a shingle mill built in 1849. Mining started in 1850.

Coloma

This is where it all began. On a cold January morning in 1848, James Marshall picked up a few flakes of gold from a mill race and started the Gold Rush that changed the history of a nation and the economy of a whole planet.

Emmanuel Episcopal Church, shown here, and Catholic Church are among Coloma's oldest buildings.

THE APPEALING, APPALLING MR. SUTTER

The discovery of gold in Coloma gave John Sutter a golden opportunity to become one of the greatest men in California history. Instead, it ruined him. By 1852, he had lost all of the land and prestige that had taken years to develop, and he had to leave California a bankrupt and broken man.

Sutter's career is full of contradictions. In many ways, he was one of the most appealing of the California pioneers, and his settling of the interior valley was one of the most important milestones in the state's history. On the other hand, many aspects of his personal life are downright appalling, and most of his problems were the direct result of his own irresponsibility.

John August Sutter was born Johann Augustus Suter in Switzerland in 1803. He married at the age of 23, fathered a family, ran up a tremendous list of debts, and was able to avoid debtors' prison only by abandoning his family and escaping to America. Sutter spent five years traveling through the West and building a fraudulent reputation as a military captain and a man of means, and then set out for California via Oregon, Alaska, and Hawaii. He arrived in Monterey in 1839 and boldly announced plans to establish a great colony.

Sutter, with a small group of white men and Hawaiians (including a couple of mistresses), picked a spot for his colony where the American River joined the Sacramento. He cleared land, planted orchards and crops, started livestock herds, and pushed back the wilderness. He named his empire New Helvetia, after the ancient title of his fatherland.

In 1841, Sutter bought Fort Ross from the Russians in an attempt to expand his empire. But the purchase turned out to be a costly mistake. Sutter had very little money to begin with, and operated almost entirely on credit. The Fort Ross purchase brought his debts to the critical point, and crop failures in 1843 added to the load. To keep himself going, he mortgaged his property, faulted on payments to the Russians, forged checks, and sold his Indian slaves. He somehow managed to stay solvent, and at the same time acted as California's most gracious host. Immigrants and visiting dignitaries found him to be very generous, and the self-styled land baron developed a reputation as a magnanimous man of means. No one realized that Sutter actually lived a very precarious existence.

After Marshall discovered gold in the tail race of the partially-completed mill, Sutter naively asked all his men to keep the event a secret so he could get some lumber cut and sold. At the same time, he tried to acquire mineral rights to the Coloma land. But the rights weren't granted, the news of the discovery leaked out, and Sutter lost his big chance. Miners divided the Coloma lands to suit themselves, and Sutter was powerless to do anything to stop them. Squatters even carved up New Helvetia.

Sutter's greatest benefits from the Gold Rush came from renting the fort buildings to merchants. However, he used the income to finance a period of wild carousing instead of paying his debts. Like James Marshall, Sutter believed he had some divine right to a share of all the

Hero or heel?

gold coming out of the foothills and that he would enjoy an endless source of income.

Stories about Sutter, both as a wealthy do-gooder and a debt-ridden despot, reached Europe and one of his sons decided to visit New Helvetia to get the facts. Young Augustus Sutter found his father in a scandalous situation, living the high life while the debts mounted ever higher. In a legal move to thwart Russian attempts to dispossess Sutter, all of New Helvetia was transferred into the son's name. Then the father left Augustus at the fort to face the creditors, and went off on a wild spree in the mines.

Young Sutter saved his father from destruction. At the suggestion of Sam Brannan, he founded a new city named Sacramento, and used the income from the land sales to pay the debts. The fort was sold to raise more money and Sutter and Son moved their headquarters to a hock farm on the Feather River. Since the finances were now in good shape, young Sutter sent for his mother and sister. But before they could arrive, the father somehow managed to get control of the land and money away from his son. When his family landed in California, they found the aging John in the position of a successful country gentleman with almost unlimited income from land sales. In 1850, Augustus left for Mexico, and with him went all semblance of order in the household. Sutter's extravagances got the better of him again, and within a year he had lost all of his property and business interests except the hock farm. Even that had to be mortgaged to pay for lawyers, taxes, interest on loans, and personal expenses.

Sutter tried to claim payments for some of his lost lands, but the courts ruled that most of the original land grants were invalid. Without any means of support, Sutter retired to his farm to live a despondent life. He and his wife fled when squatters burned down their ranch house, and moved East. They settled in Lititz, Pennsylvania, where Sutter died on June 18, 1880.

Sutter's Fort was restored by the State of California in 1891-1893, and it is still one of the best historical museums in California. Mementos of Sutter's life are carefully preserved, and his achievements are duly noted for all schoolchildren to admire. Though he dissipated great opportunities and great fortunes, John Sutter is destined to remain one of California's most popular heroes.

Noisy stamp mills such as this one at Coloma were used to crush the gold-bearing quartz taken from mines.

First miners used pan and primitive cradle to get gold from the banks of the American River.

Naturally, Coloma was the first of the mining boom towns. By summer of 1848, there were 2,000 miners living on the banks of the river, and the population swelled to 10,000 during the next year. Virtually all of the new miners in the foothills started out at Coloma before branching out to the newer strikes. It was here that Gold Rush inflation hit the hardest. Picks and shovels sold for $50 each and foodstuffs went for astronomical prices.

This may have been the first boom town, but it certainly wasn't the longest lived. By 1852, there wasn't much gold left and a good part of the population moved on to more golden pastures.

On the grisly side, Coloma was the scene of one of the Gold Country's most celebrated double hangings in 1855.

The principles were Mickey Free and Dr. Crane. Mickey Free was a badman — a robber and a murderer the law had finally caught up with in Placerville. Dr. Crane, a teacher, had been convicted of dispatching one of his pupils, a young lady named Susan who had been foolish enough to reject his proposal of marriage.

The town made quite an affair of the proceedings. There was a brass band from Placerville and the crowd

Sutter's sawmill has been reconstructed in Coloma; it was in the tailrace of original that Marshall found gold.

WHERE DID EVERYBODY COME FROM?

In the spring of 1848 — after Marshall's discovery but before the actual Gold Rush had really started — there were less than 15,000 people in California, not counting the uncountable Indians. A state census in 1852 revealed that the non-Indian population had swelled to almost 225,000. Where did all the people come from?

Historians estimate that about 65 to 75 per cent came from other parts of the United States. Some 100,000 miners came to California from the East via overland routes during the first three years of the Gold Rush, and the rest either braved the long ocean voyage around the Horn, or went through the agonies of combining two ocean voyages with the often miserable trip across the Isthmus of Panama.

Of the 25 to 35 per cent of the Argonauts who came from outside the United States, the most noticeable influx during the first two or three years was from Latin America. Mexicans — particularly those from the state of Sonora — and Chileans were among the first to hear about the discovery of gold in California, and they swarmed northward to share the wealth. An estimated 5,000 Chileans arrived in California during the first six months of 1849, and the number of Mexicans was even higher. It is difficult to obtain an accurate count of the Mexicans, since they did not stay in California during the winter, but chose instead to commute back and forth so they could work in the mines during the dry season was in a holiday mood. But it was the fact that both the and return to their homes when the rains arrived to make mining impractical.

Of the European countries, the British Isles produced the greatest number of Argonauts. Potato famine, economic depression, and social upheavals prompted English, Scots, Irish, and Welsh to give up their homes and make the long voyage to California. Many of them brought valuable mining experience to the new gold fields.

The second greatest contributor was Germany, where political revolution and crop losses prompted emigration in search of wealth and a new life. France, too, lost several thousand to the Gold Rush, because of political instability and depression. A few thousand Scandinavians joined the Rush.

The Chinese got a late start, but quickly made up for lost time. In 1850 — when the Europeans and Latin Americans were arriving in droves — there were still only 600 Chinese in California. By 1852, their numbers had grown to 25,000. It is interesting to note that the Japanese did not participate in the Gold Rush at all, since emigration was frowned upon at that time.

While exact figures on immigration are hard to determine because of contradictions and duplications in census reports, it is clear that the California Gold Rush was an international event. And this world-wide drawing power was to have a profound effect on the future population distribution throughout the state.

---

was in a holiday mood. But it was the fact that both the doomed came through in the spirit of the occasion that made it a truly memorable event.

With the noose around his neck, Dr. Crane sang several verses of a song he had composed as his departing message and topped off the performance with the shout, "Here I come, Susan!" as the trap fell.

Mickey Free, not to be outdone, rounded out the show with an improvised jig, and then unwittingly climaxed the day by writhing to his death by strangulation after the noose had slipped and failed to snap his neck. His gravestone is still visible in the Coloma cemetery.

Coloma is preserved in a state park, and several buildings are marked for easy identification. Rangers on duty in the museum can provide a detailed map of the park, showing all points of interest.

By far the most imposing structure in Coloma is the reconstruction of Sutter's Mill, which was completed in January, 1968. It wasn't possible to rebuild the mill on the exact location of the original, since the American River has altered its course substantially. But the rebuilders were able to follow the original construction techniques right down to the hand-hewn beams and mortise-and-tenon joints.

Among the most notable Gold Rush buildings to be seen here are Beakert's Store and Gunsmith Shop, the Chinese stone buildings, ruins of the Bell Store, and the Episcopal and Catholic churches.

On the hill behind the old town, an imposing bronze statue of James Marshall points to the site of the gold discovery. On the road down from the statue is the Marshall Cabin, where he lived until 1868.

One of the best views of the Coloma Valley is from the Mt. Murphy Road (unpaved). At one time, there was a cannon on top of the hill that was used to signal the arrival of stagecoaches.

Lotus

Now off the beaten trail, Lotus lives a quiet existence with only a few reminders of the early days. The old schoolhouse, opened in 1869, has enjoyed a rebirth as an art gallery. There is also the crumbling ruins of the brick Lohry General Store, and the small Uniontown Pioneer Cemetery up on the hill.

WHERE DID EVERYBODY GO?

At the peak of the Gold Rush, some 120,000 miners were busy digging for gold in the California foothills. By 1873, the total was down to 30,000 — and more than half of them were persistent Chinese who laboriously reworked the gravels that weren't worth anyone else's efforts. Where did everybody go?

There is no way of arriving at any exact counts since the miners drifted away over a long period, and not many left their forwarding addresses. But without trying to grasp at figures, it is not difficult to list their probable destinations.

First of all, a lot of the miners went home. Some were disillusioned either by wild stories of streets paved with gold or by their own daydreams, and the hard realities of mining were a great disappointment. Others went back home because of persecution. This is particularly true of the Latin Americans, Frenchmen, and Chinese. Hard-nosed Yankees who ran the "furriners" out of the best diggin's and even out of some towns were bad enough. But the cruelest blow was the vindictive Foreign Miners Tax adopted in 1850. All miners who were not citizens had to pay $20 a month for the privilege of mining, and their permits had to be renewed on a monthly basis. This was a bitter pill for the Mexicans who had been among the first to arrive in the gold fields and who had taught the Yankees how to pan the gravels.

Another group of the Gold Rush miners was virtually without home or nationality. They followed wherever fortune beckoned, and left California in search of new El Dorados — in Nevada, Montana, Australia, British Columbia, or anywhere else that promised overnight fortunes. Nothing could have held this bunch in one place except a limitless supply of rumors and misty promises.

Fortunately for California, a good many of the Argonauts decided to stay in the state, even after their dreams of instant wealth had been shattered. There was plenty to do, and no lack of variety in occupations. Some of the miners stayed right in the gold fields, and went to work for the big commercial quartz and hydraulic operations that thrived for another thirty years. Others found employment in peripheral industries that supplied the mines —mills, iron foundries and machine shops.

Those who had adopted mining just because of its get-rich-quick aspects returned to their old professions. After 1860, California began to evolve from a mining state to one based on agriculture, stock raising, lumbering, and commerce. Former farmers and dairymen easily found work in the California valleys and settled down there. Office workers moved into the cities, particularly San Francisco but also Sacramento and Stockton.

Not many of the Argonauts really got rich from the Gold Rush. But many of them found a new life in California, and stayed around to make notable contributions to the rapid economic growth of the state.

Pilot Hill

The only building of interest in this old mining town is the three-story Bayley House, which stands beside State Route 49. Originally planned as a hotel to take care of the people who were supposed to travel on the railroad that was supposed to pass within half a mile of Pilot Hill, the building became "Bayley's Folly" when the Central Pacific chose another route at the last minute.

Alonzo Bayley finished the house in 1862 and tried to operate it anyway, but never enjoyed any success. The building was sold several times during the next 50 years and even operated as headquarters of a cattle ranch. Today it stands padlocked and unused as a stately reminder of a dream that collapsed.

Greenwood

Greenwood was established by an old trapper, John Greenwood, and his two sons who set up store in 1848 when they found that providing supplies to the hungry miners was more reliable than digging in the cold stream beds. The town grew to respectable proportions in the early years and boasted among other things a well-attended theater. The surrounding countryside is covered with orchards, and Greenwood has managed to carry on as a tiny trading center.

Georgetown

One of the first things that strikes visitors to Georgetown is the inordinately wide main street that splits the old town. It is wide indeed — a full 100 feet — and it was designed that way as fire protection after a blaze leveled the original tent city in 1852. Even the side streets are wider than usual — 60 feet — just to keep fire from jumping from block to block.

Georgetown has other notable features. There are a few small stores and a brick I.O.O.F. Hall on the main street that date back to the late 1850's, and some old-fashioned country places and big gardens that were built later in the nineteenth century. At its peak, Georgetown was called the "Pride of the Mountains," and some of the old character is still preserved today.

Georgetown got its start in 1849 when George Phipps and a party of sailors worked the stream below

Old schoolhouse in Lotus has been refurbished and converted into a popular gallery for local artists.

Quaint old Georgetown residence was built in the 1860's, has somehow managed to avoid fires since then.

Covered sidewalks flank the wide main street of Georgetown that was devised to halt the spread of fire.

the present townsite and struck it rich. The camp was first named Growlersburg, because the nuggets growled in the miners' pans. Tents became the most popular form of architecture, and the streets were lined with miners shacks and canvas meeting halls. But in 1852 a photographer trying to take a picture of a dead miner in a gambling hall started a fire and the whole town was leveled. It was then that the wide streets were laid out and the town was rebuilt on a more solid scale. By 1855, there were 3,000 people enjoying the cultural life that included events at a town hall and theater.

Georgetown even had a good garden nursery that helped build the town into a tree-shaded and flowered family settlement. It is said that the original plants from this nursery gave rise to the spectacular display of wild Scotch broom that covers the hillsides around Georgetown and Greenwood every spring.

Garden Valley

This early mining camp originally was named Johnstown after a sailor who first struck it rich. But when the

Long Tom was used by miners to work the gravels of Spanish Flat, short-lived mining camp near Kelsey.

Leaky flume near Georgetown is reminiscent of time when hundreds of miles of troughs laced Gold Country.

placers had been worked out, residents turned to truck farming and changed the name appropriately.

Kelsey

Kelseys Diggings, as it was first known, is all but dead and there is little remaining to suggest that this was once one of the rowdiest of the gold camps, with six hotels and 24 saloons. There is a marker showing the site of James Marshall's Blacksmith Shop, and a poorly maintained sign at the site of the Union Hotel where he died in 1885.

Volcanoville

At last count, there were two permanent residents in Volcanoville, a tiny mountain town that enjoyed a brief period of glory in the 1850's when its auriferous gravels were productive. But Volcanoville had no other reason for existence, so the end of the gold meant the end of the town. A fire in 1907 leveled all but a few of its Gold Rush buildings. The only authentic relic of the 1850's is a small bar at the end of the road.

Short, sad story is told on a gravestone in the tiny cemetery on the seldom-traveled road to Volcanoville.

Finding gold in the California foothills depended a great deal on luck. Getting the gold out of the ground depended on hard, back-breaking work. Gold mining was not an easy task, and many of the miners who eagerly traveled to the gold fields expecting to pick up nuggets off the ground turned away disillusioned when they realized the amount of hard labor required to get a day's wages.

It is true that some of the miners were able to pick up free gold, chisel nuggets out of crevices with a pocket knife, and get thousands of dollars worth of dust in a single pan. But these joys belonged only to a few who were lucky enough to be the first to strike some very rich diggin's. Their followers rarely were able to share this quick wealth, and were forced to work harder for less money and dream of the day when they would be the first to discover a new bonanza.

Mining evolved from a one-man operation into a big business. The stereotype of the California miner was a solitary figure, kneeling at the edge of a stream and panning carefully while birds sang overhead and his burro browsed contentedly. But this miner represented only the beginning, and he wasn't able to survive long in the intense competition that developed.

PANNING FOR GOLD. Panning was the simplest way to separate gold from dirt and rocks. The basic procedure was to shovel some gold-bearing materials into a shallow pan, add some water, and then carefully swirl the mixture around so the water and light material spilled over the side and the heavy stuff — including gold — settled to the bottom of the pan (see page 49).

Gold panning techniques are centuries-old, and they were put to use in the southern United States several decades before the California Gold Rush. It is believed that Isaac Humphrey, a Georgian, was the first to introduce gold panning at Coloma in 1848. But the Mexicans also had developed the skills in their own country, using a flat dish called a *batea*.

The trouble with panning was its slowness. About 20 minutes was needed to wash a single pan and pick up the fine particles of gold. On a good day, one miner could only wash about 50 pans.

ROCKING THE CRADLE. Isaac Humphrey also introduced the rocker or cradle to the California gold fields. A rocker was simply a rectangular wooden box, set on a slope and mounted on rockers. At the top was a sieve, and at the bottom was a series of cleats or riffles. The dirt was poured into the top, followed by a bucket of water. The cradle was rocked to agitate the mixture and send it flowing through the box. The big rocks were caught in the sieve, the waste ran out the lower end with the water, and the heavy gold fell to the bottom of the box and was caught on the cleats.

The rocker had many advantages. It could be made quickly and moved from site to site. Since water was added by the bucketful, no continuous source was needed, and the rocker became popular at the "dry diggin's"

where water had to be carried by hand. But the main advantage was that one miner could wash a lot more dirt with a cradle than he could with a pan, and two men working together could wash a cubic yard a day.

The rocker and the gold pan worked reasonably well for coarse gold, but were inefficient at trapping the fine particles or "flour" gold. To increase their take from each load, miners began adding small amounts of mercury to the bottom of the cradle. Mercury has the unique ability to trap fine gold while refusing almost everything else. Periodically, the miners would remove the mercury and heat it; the mercury would vaporize, leaving behind the free gold.

The Long Tom was an enlarged, modified cradle. It consisted of a 10-to-20-foot trough, about a foot wide, fitted with a sheet of perforated metal. Underneath this sheet was located the riffle box. At least two men shoveled the pay dirt into the top of the Long Tom. The third man in the crew threw out the big rocks as they collected and kept the pay dirt moving along through the box. Once or twice a day, the gold and sand caught on the riffles would be removed and panned.

The Long Tom could handle a lot of dirt, but it needed a continuous source of fast-moving water. This meant that the miners either had to locate right on the bank of a river or dig ditches to bring the water to the site of rich but dry dirt. The first mining ditch in the Gold Rush Country was supposedly built in 1850 to supply the Long Toms working near Nevada City.

SLUICING. Sluice boxes were longer versions of the Long Tom, built on the theory that more gold would precipitate if the length of the riffle boxes was extended. A number of sluice boxes were often fastened together in a long line, and a whole crew of miners was kept busy shoveling dirt and gravel into the troughs.

Ground sluicing was practiced in a number of ways. One was to dig a shallow ditch and divert river water into it to soften the soil. The miners would then dig at the dirt and rock with picks and let the water carry the loosened material down a sluice box stationed at the bottom of the ditch. The gold was finally removed from the sluice boxes by panning.

HYDRAULIC MINING. Hydraulic mining was the most efficient method of getting gold out of the ground, but it was also the most destructive to the countryside (see page 78). The operating principle was very simple: if water under pressure could be directed against a bank of soft gravels, the bank would disintegrate very rapidly and the dirt would wash downhill into a series of huge sluice boxes that would catch the gold.

Hydraulicking was introduced in California in 1853 by E. E. Matteson, a Nevada City miner. His was a very simple operation, with a small volume of water carried through a canvas hose and spewed forth through a primitive nozzle fabricated out of sheet metal. Enterprising miners quickly saw the possibilities of hydraulicking, and procedures became more sophisticated. Iron pipe and

HOW THE CALIFORNIA MINES ARE WORKED.

Composite drawing shows common forms of mining.

Awkward gold dredge processed gravel by the ton.

good hoses replaced the canvas, and big nozzles were fabricated under the names of Monitor and Giant.

The key to hydraulicking was a constant source of water. Some of the big nozzles were nine inches in diameter and required 30,000 gallons of water a minute. To get the water to the mining sites, very expensive systems of flumes and ditches had to be dug. It is estimated that by 1859, some 5,000 miles of canals and viaducts stretched across the countryside, particularly in the Northern Mines. Single lines were as much as 15 or 20 miles long. The water line always came into the mining area at a high elevation, so that a natural drop of 100 to 400 feet would generate enough force to build up high pressure at the nozzle.

The power of a hydraulic nozzle is hard to describe. One historian compares it with turning a modern fire hose on a sand pile or a bank of snow. Whole mountain slopes could be devoured in a day, with the gravels rushing down through the sluices and out into piles of waste. It was this waste or "slickin's" that led to the downfall of hydraulic mining. It clogged the rivers and was carried down into the farmlands where it caused floods, disrupted agriculture, and even discolored San Francisco Bay. The miners were ordered to quit hydraulicking unless they could dispose of the waste; this was impossible so the method was abandoned.

Despite the high volumes of gravel that could be mined by hydraulicking, the system was not very efficient and a lot of gold got away in the fast-moving water that poured through the sluices. The tailings were rich enough to warrant another mining, and enterprising miners working behind the hydraulickers often did very well.

DREDGING. Wherever there was enough water to float them, big dredgers could be used to work deep gold-bearing gravels. Buckets could dig up material as much as 100 feet below the water level and dump it into a floating processing plant. The gravel was screened, jiggled, and washed to separate rock from gold and sand. The heavy material was finally forced into barrels where copper plates covered with mercury trapped the gold. The waste was pumped out the rear of the dredger into huge piles that forever ruined the land for any other purpose.

Dredging was first tried in the 1850's but it did not become popular — or profitable — until the early 1900's.

The last gold dredger (the largest one ever built) was still working near Hammonton in 1968.

DRIFT MINING. The deep gravels of ancient river channels often held a good supply of gold. To get at it, the miners would sink shafts called "coyote holes" straight down until they hit pay dirt, and then dig horizontal tunnels or "drifts" along the richest deposits.

The trouble was, the best deposits were at the bottom of the gravel near bed rock. So the shafts usually had to be sunk deep into the ground — a very time-consuming, dangerous, and expensive operation. Gravel just below the surface of the ground could be shoveled out, but windlasses with buckets had to be rigged for deep digging. The shafts built in the 1850's did not have proper framing, and cave-ins were frequent and disastrous.

QUARTZ MINING. It was with hard-rock quartz operations that gold mining in California became a business rather than an adventure. The first quartz mine in California was opened in 1849 at Mariposa, but this system hit its peak in the Northern Mines, particularly around Grass Valley (see page 74).

Digging the gold-bearing quartz out of the mountains was done with gunpowder and picks and shovels. Miners from England and Wales were instrumental in adapting their Old-Country mining techniques to California and in teaching inexperienced miners how to find the best veins and then follow them. Fortunately, many of the deposits were shallow so the mines consisted more of horizontal tunnels than vertical shafts.

Once the ore was brought above ground, it had to be crushed. The first crushing equipment was the Mexican *arrastra,* a primitive arrangement that pulverized the rock between a stationary stone slab and a moving stone slab that was drawn in a circle by mule or manpower. The best crusher was the vertical stamp mill, adapted from European designs. The hammers of these big stamps were lifted by steam and dropped by gravity in a noisy rotation that pounded the ore into workable dust.

Separating the gold from the pulverized ore proved to be a problem. The old mercury methods didn't work well with this type of ore because of contaminants. After several wasteful experiments, a chemical process using chlorine gas was devised that worked adequately.

Auburn's Old Town has many original Gold Rush buildings, including a block of remodeled structures (shown above) on Commercial street that are inhabited by modern businessmen who preserve the old-time feeling.

THE AUBURN AREA

AUBURN • OPHIR • FOREST HILL • YANKEE JIMS • MICHIGAN BLUFF
IOWA HILL • GOLD RUN • DUTCH FLAT

Auburn

In the spring of 1848, Claude Chana and a party of Indians decided to leave the diggings at Coloma and see if they could find their own strike in the hills to the northwest. They discovered one of the richest surface deposits in the Gold Country and settled what is today the city of Auburn.

During the summer of that year, the gravels at North Fork Dry Diggings, as the camp was first named, yielded great wealth to those who took the effort to cart the paydirt to the stream below. It was common-place for a miner to wash out $1,000 to $1,500 a day. One account tells of four or five cart loads producing $16,000 in a single day. By 1850, 1,500 miners were digging in Auburn Ravine.

But the surface placers were quickly exhausted, and it took an accidental discovery to keep the town booming.

A miner named Jenkins had built a ditch and flume to carry water to his claim in Missouri Gulch. A week after he had finished, the water mysteriously ceased to flow. He investigated, and found that the water was pouring into a gopher hole on the flat above the claim.

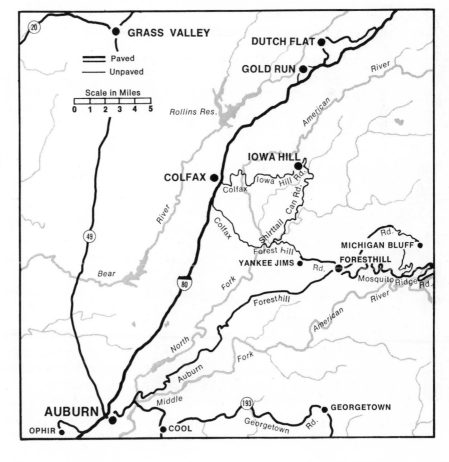

Major mining camps are accessible via side roads that branch off Interstate 80. The road between Yankee Jims and Iowa Hill is unpaved, but passable in dry weather.

Hanging yard used by early Auburnites is now covered by the imposing Placer County Courthouse.

Old town plaza in Auburn shows a strong Spanish influence. Striped building is the four-story firehouse.

Women were few and far between in the early mining camps. This sturdy soul is visiting miners in Auburn Ravine.

Looking closely, he saw that the bottom of the ditch was covered with coarse gold. In a month, Jenkins took over $40,000 and Auburn's future was fixed.

It wasn't gold that built the modern city you find today, however. From the very earliest days, Auburn's location has made it a natural transportation center. Both a major transcontinental highway and the Southern Pacific Railroad pass through Auburn.

The modern section of Auburn is built on top of a hill. The Old Town, with its collection of Gold Rush buildings, lies below and west of the imposing county courthouse. Because the business district in Auburn has migrated up the hill over the years, the early buildings have been left relatively uncovered and untrammeled by modern commerce.

You can see all the noteworthy buildings on a short walk along Lincoln Way, Court Street, and Commercial Street. Look for the square, four-story firehouse, the Wells Fargo Office that is now a gift shop, the post office that opened in 1849, and a whole block full of attractively decorated offices and shops.

The Placer County Courthouse is not really a Gold Rush building, having been finished in the 1890's, but it is located on the early public square that served as the first public hanging yard and graveyard for the town. Nearby is the Methodist Church built in 1858.

The Placer County Museum, at the fairgrounds, has several interesting exhibits including replicas of rooms from homes built and used during the early mining days, and displays of Chinese and Indian objects from the same era.

Ophir

The richest diggings around Auburn were in the ravine west of town. Several camps grew up there during the 1850's including Frytown, Virginiatown, Gold Hill, Spanish Corral. The only one that is still recognizable is Spanish Corral, which was renamed as Ophir when it reigned as the largest town in Placer County and an important quartz-mining center. Now, it is only a quiet crossroad. A marker, erected in 1950, describes the old town. Fires and the erosion of time have destroyed all remnants of the Gold Rush.

Forest Hill

Forest Hill, on the ridge between Shirttail Canyon and the middle fork of the American River, was a prosperous mining and trading center during the early 1850's. Gold was first discovered in 1850, but the boom did not really start until the Jenny Lind mine was opened in 1852. This famous mine alone produced over a million dollars in gold by 1880, and the area around Forest Hill produced in excess of $10 million.

One of the best-preserved hydraulic nozzles in the Gold Country is on display near the firehouse. The small collection of old businesses is fronted by wooden sidewalks with the traditional overhangs.

Yankee Jims

Yankee Jims sprang into being under strange circumstances, but the story is a credible one.

Yankee Jim, who was not, in fact, a Yankee but an Australian, was a low character. Rather than dig and wash the good soil of the American River, he stole horses. And nothing was lower than a horse thief in those day. Horse thieves, if caught, were summarily strung up.

Yankee Jim was an old professional, and if one of his victims hadn't bothered to make a careful investigation, the old boy might have gone on indefinitely. But the victim found his horse, and others, too, in a corral hidden away in a high and remote part of a ridge. Yankee Jim hightailed it out of the country just in time to save his neck, and in a way it was sort of a shame.

Weathered cemeteries such as this one at Iowa Hill are often the most revealing links with the past.

A single marker and tiny Wells Fargo Office tell the story of Iowa Hill's great prosperity in the 1850's.

Dutch Flat Hotel was built in 1852 by Charles Steffens, and was one of two that served the town during good times.

In addition to the IOOF and Masonic halls shown here, Dutch Flat also boasted an opera house and three schools.

Union Church in Gold Run stands among man-made canyons that were dug by ambitious hydraulic miners.

Because it wasn't much later that a miner wandered into the old corral to do a bit of prospecting and found the ground was rich in free gold.

A crowded camp mushroomed up and a fortune was taken from the diggings — a fortune that could have been Jim's, if it had occurred to him to try his hand at a little honest labor.

Yankee Jims grew into Placer County's largest mining camp; today, you'll find only a few weathered structures.

Michigan Bluff

Best remembered for the extensive hydraulic mining which tore away at the mountainsides in the area, Michigan Bluff consists today of a few frame buildings left from the 1880's when the Monitors were muzzled. Between 1853 and 1858, approximately $100,000 in bullion was shipped from the region each month.

Michigan City, which was the original town site half a mile away, had its foundations undermined by furious hydraulicking during those five years, so in 1859 the population moved *en masse* to a location higher on the brow of Sugar Loaf Hill. They called the new camp Michigan Bluff.

NOW LET'S ALL JOIN HANDS...

One of the things that impresses visitors to the Gold Country is the disproportionately high number of lodge hall buildings that are still standing. An IOOF or Masonic Hall frequently is the most conspicuous ruin in a small town that has been ravaged by fire, and both lodge buildings are almost always included in the best-preserved mining communities. These buildings not only attest to the wise building practices of the lodge founders, but they are also important reflections of an important Gold Rush phenomenon — the need for companionship.

The strongest of the fraternal organizations in the eastern United States — particularly the Odd Fellows and the Masons — sanctioned California lodges early in 1849 to help any of the brethren who might get in trouble far from home. These lodges were badly needed, since many of the men who went broke, got sick, or died were without friends or any source of financial aid.

The fraternities quickly spread through the gold fields, and new lodges opened with each new strike. Organizers had very little trouble recruiting new members, since the lonely miners leaped at every chance to join their fellow men and establish some comradeship to help overcome the lonely life in the mines. Those who struck it rich gave freely to building programs, with the result that the lodge halls were made of stone and brick while many other buildings were wood and canvas. Meetings were well-attended, and the local lodge was often the charitable backbone of the community.

When the gold gave out, so did the lodge charters. Hundreds or thousands of members would vanish overnight, many to reappear again on the rolls of some new lodge in some new boom town. When fire came to the abandoned towns — and it always did — the flimsy buildings burned in a wink while the lodge halls and similarly constructed buildings stood their ground. After a century, they are still proud reminders of the wisdom of their builders.

There was one fraternity that didn't quite fit this mold. E Clampus Vitus was founded in 1850 by J. H. Zumwalt of Mokelumne Hill, a man of good humor who decided that the solemn and mysterious fraternal organizations could do with a bit of needling. E Clampus Vitus was a fraternity for non-joiners. It existed only for the purpose of taking in new members, all of whom were held in an office of equal indignity and were ruled by a Noble Grand Humbug. Members were pledged to a life of jollity and informality, and developed such a comradely spirit that a man would have a hard time doing business in many communities if he were not a member.

With all the partying and joking, the Clampers managed to do some good work helping the needy. The charity was always anonymous, but the many letters of thanks printed in the newspapers of the day attest to the regard in which the pranksters were held.

E Clampus Vitus was revived in the 1930's, and several historical markers erected by modern Clampers can be spotted in the Gold Country.

Iowa Hill

Gold wasn't discovered here until 1853, but there was enough to keep the area thriving until 1858. More than $20 million was taken from the ridge on which the town sits.

The Wells Fargo Vault is the only link with this monied past. Fires have been part of Iowa Hill's history since 1857, when the original town was burned to ashes. The last fire was in 1922.

As with many other Gold Country towns, the pioneer cemetery on Banjo Hill provides the most stirring touch with the past.

Gold Run

Rich deposits of gold-bearing gravel along an ancient stream bed enabled Gold Run to boom right up to the court-imposed end of hydraulic mining in 1884. The town was founded by O. W. Hollenbeck in 1854 and was first called Mountain Springs. The real rich times arrived with the hydraulic mining operations in 1859.

Only the little shingled Union Church, with its shiny new roof, is a memento of the old days. The church was one of many buildings in the Gold Country financed by miners' contributions.

Dutch Flat

Dutch Flat is one of the most lovable old towns in the Northern Mines. It has a number of significant old buildings, plus some very pleasant residential areas that give the town a special character.

A German miner, Joseph Dorenbach, and his countrymen started washing the gravels around Dutch Flat in 1851. From 1854 to 1883, the town was one of the principal placer mining towns in the state.

Dutch Flat is one of the few Gold Country towns that has not suffered a serious fire, and this blessing shows up in the concentration of century-old buildings along the main street, including the old hotel, I.O.O.F. and Masonic Halls, Methodist Church, and Runckel Home.

Until the railroad had pushed its way up to Cisco, Dutch Flat was an important stage stop on both the Donner Pass and Henness Pass routes. At the height of its prosperity, the town supported two hotels and dozens of other businesses.

Giant Pelton Wheel in Grass Valley's Boston Ravine has been quiet for more than 30 years. When the quartz mines were working, the wheel whipped around at 70 miles an hour to produce power.

THE GRASS VALLEY AREA

GRASS VALLEY • ROUGH AND READY • FRENCH CORRAL • SMARTVILLE

TIMBUCTOO • NORTH SAN JUAN • NEVADA CITY • WASHINGTON

NORTH BLOOMFIELD • RELIEF HILL

Grass Valley

Grass Valley may well be the most important gold mining town in all of California. The town has kept pace with the changes of modern life, so very little feeling of Gold Rush days can be found today. Still, it was here that gold mining hit its peak as an industry. This was not a legendary ground where grizzled miners found big nuggets, but it was the area where big money and big machinery moved in to take as much gold as efficiently as possible. The most important "ruins" left around Grass Valley are not small brick businesses or quaint Chinese quarters, but the head frames and inclined elevators of the big mining complexes that once employed thousands of miners.

When the big mining companies moved in, they attracted the important suppliers and peripheral industries, so Grass Valley possessed a broad economic base that was very rare in the Gold Country. The business of deep quartz mining was developed here, and the hit-and-miss methods of adventurous prospecting were re-

placed by industrial techniques that required brains and know-how instead of luck and brawn.

The first big strike, however, came about much as it did in many other gold camps—just by accident. The surface diggings in this area were not rich, so only a few of 1849's frenzied prospectors even bothered to set up camp. One of those who did try his luck on the edges of Boston Ravine was George Knight, and he was destined to change the area's fortune overnight.

The story goes that Knight was out chasing his wandering cow in the moonlight when he stubbed his toe on a rocky outcropping. The stumble knocked loose a piece of rock, and Knight noticed the glitter of shining metal. He forgot about his cow, took the piece of rock home and crushed it. A few minutes' work with the gold pan revealed that the rock was gold-bearing quartz, not the first discovered in the Gold Country but by far the most important.

The news of Knight's discovery brought miners in droves, and by summer, the Gold Hill Company had built a mill near the point where the toe-stubbing took

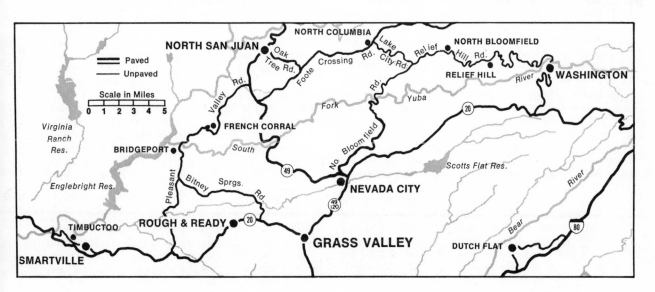

Grass Valley and Nevada City will soon be linked by freeway. Side road through French Corral is partially unpaved. Dirt road from Washington to Relief Hill is only for experienced mountain drivers.

place. Other companies followed and within a mile or two of town could be found the Empire, North Star, Pennsylvania, Idaho-Maryland, Brunswick, and others. Hundreds of miles of tunnels and shafts were dug beneath Grass Valley and its neighbor, Nevada City, and mining continued well into the 1950's. You can get the feel of these busy mining days by visiting the sites of the old mines (see page 74). Just the very size of the surface buildings gives a good idea of the scope of this town's mining boom.

A huge fire in 1855 — probably the most disastrous of the many that ravaged Gold Rush camps — destroyed the 300-odd frame buildings that made up the original community of Grass Valley. The most famous residential building left in town is identified with Lola Montez. Other buildings of historical note include the Glasson Home at 515 Main Street, the Matteson Home at 318 Neal Street, The Tremoreaux Home at 403 Neal Street, the Watt Home at 506 Linden Avenue, and the Bourn Mansion at the Empire Mine.

LOLA AND LOTTA...A FLASHY PAIR OF QUEENS

There are no more famous names in the history of the Northern Mines than those of Lola Montez and Lotta Crabtree. They injected an element of glamour into the often tawdry routine of the mining camps, and stories about this flashy pair of queens are easy to come by and often repeated.

Lola Montez — born Eliza Gilbert in Ireland in 1818 — was a sensation in Europe during the 1840's, both for her theatrical talents and her personal life. She was the mistress of Ludwig of Bavaria for two years and later presided over soirees where the Continent's foremost literary and artistic figures held sway. Franz Liszt, George Sand, Victor Hugo, and Alexander Dumas were among her intimates.

Lola embarked on a tour of America in 1852 and eventually made it to San Francisco the following year. Her famous beauty and notoriety packed the audiences, but her mediocre dancing talents—even in the exotic Spider Dance—were somewhat disappointing to the jaded San Franciscans. She received an even harsher reception at performances in Sacramento and Marysville, and finally descended on Grass Valley where she decided to forsake the theater and retire. She moved into the house on Mill Street that is still standing today and set up a sort of housekeeping that included keeping grizzly bears and monkeys as pets, throwing big parties, and giving occasional performances for local crowds.

Among the most famous — and least credible — stories about Lola Montez had her performing her provocative, miniskirted dance at the door of an objecting minister and horsewhipping a newspaper editor for printing some inaccuracy about her.

When not living the high life, Lola stayed around the house and even managed to get a garden started. Schoolchildren passed her house regularly, and one day, little 7-year-old Lotta Crabtree stopped by for a visit. The Crabtrees lived just down the block from the Montez house, and Lola and Lotta became good friends. The bubbling, irrepressible little girl caught the aging beauty's fancy, and Lola began to teach her little friend some songs and dances. Lotta learned very quickly and was soon performing for Miss Montez's guests. Legend has it that Lola took the little girl with her on a trip to Rough and Ready, and Lotta gave her first public performance on top of the anvil in Fippin's Smithy while

Lola, the teacher.   Lotta, the student.

the talented blacksmith pounded out accompaniment with his hammer.

In 1854 — about a year after Lola and Lotta first met — the Crabtrees moved to La Porte. Student and teacher were separated, but Lotta was ready to go out on her own. She went on the stage of a local tavern at the age of 8 and was a smash success. The miners showered the stage with coins and nuggets, and Lotta was launched on a busy and very successful career. She toured the mines for years, often in grueling one-night stands, and built a huge following. Finally, she went to San Francisco for successful engagements, and then to New York in 1864 and on to international fame. She retired at an early age, and lived gracefully until 1924. At the time of her death, her estate totaled $4 million.

Fate was not so kind to her teacher. Lola Montez grew weary of "retirement" in Grass Valley and went to Australia on tour in 1855. But she failed there and returned to the United States to try her hand at lecturing, which resulted in still another failure. Her health began to give out, and once-wealthy Lola Montez spent a miserable final few years before passing away in New York at the age of 43. The year was 1861, just about the time that Lotta Crabtree was emerging as the darling of San Francisco and starting on her great career.

Lola's Grass Valley house has a spooky quality about it, hidden as it is behind gnarled trees and overgrown bushes. Its air of mystery seems to fit the former owner well. But for all her questionable qualities, it will remain to her eternal credit that Lola Montez took the time and trouble to start little Lotta Crabtree on one of the most illustrious careers in the history of the stage.

Rough and Ready has a colorful history. One of its early residents made a lot of money charging high tolls.

Old schoolhouse in Rough and Ready sits in a quiet little glen, half hidden from the main highway.

Rough and Ready

Rough and Ready is a quiet little village that belies its name. It was founded by a band of Mexican War veterans who took the name from their ex-commander, General Zachary Taylor — "Old Rough and Ready."

Rough and Ready's greatest fame comes from its secession from the Union in 1850 in protest over a miners' tax. The town actually returned to the United States after only a few months, but the rebellion was not officially ended until 1948 when peace was officially made with the federal government so a post office could be opened.

One of the town's most famous incidents reflects the temper of the Gold Rush times. It seems that an unlucky miner was being buried with a regular funeral and all the trimmings, when one of the "mourners" suddenly noticed some gold in the freshly turned earth at the gravesite. Before the preacher could finish the service, claims had been staked around the coffin and the miners had started to work.

Three of Rough and Ready's present landmarks are the old school house, the I.O.O.F. Hall, and the toll house which now houses an antique shop. North of the main highway, you'll find a fallen tree that was labeled "Slave Girl Tree" when it stood by the side of the road. According to local legend, the tree sprouted from a switch stuck in the ground by slave girl Caroline Allen while she was waiting to have her horse shod at Fippin's Smithy — which is still upright, but just barely.

French Corral

This little town was named for a Frenchman who built a corral for his mules in 1849. It enjoyed brief prosperity as a center for placer mining.

The Milton Mining and Water Company established the first cross-country phone in the state in 1877 to link its headquarters in French Corral with French Lake, 58 miles away. The brick Wells Fargo Building and the community center — originally built as a hotel and later used as a schoolhouse — both date back to the 1850's.

Two miles southwest of French Corral is a photogenic covered bridge built in 1862 at the site of the old camp of Bridgeport.

Three miles northeast of town is St. Columncille's Catholic Church, built in 1860 as training headquarters for the Bridgeport Union Guard and taken over for religious use in 1869.

Smartville

Hydraulic mining began around Smartville in the 1860's, and the town thrived until 1883. At one time there were 1,500 miners, 16 saloons, a theater, dance halls, and general stores.

The stately white Church of the Immaculate Conception, which overlooks the main road, rests on stone foundations of the original church built in 1861.

A MODERN DAY IN THE MINES

Prowling around at the Scotia Mine.

Hoist machinery at the Pennsylvania.

Getting the word at the Empire.

Thirty-stamp mill at the Gold Center Mine.

In 1967, the Grass Valley-Nevada City Kiwanis Club inaugurated an Annual Tour of the Mines, which gives visitors an unequaled opportunity to learn about the techniques of quartz mining and to take a look at some of the most important mines in the Grass Valley area.

In fact, this tour may be the only chance you have to see the famous old mines. Some are closed to the public except for this one day. Others are difficult to find unless you have a good trail of breadcrumbs to follow. And even if you can find the mines on your own, you're likely to be baffled by the function of the strange machinery that is lying around. The Kiwanis tour provides guides that serve as welcome sources of information on what the ruins are ruins of, and just what it was like back in the days when the stamp mills pounded thunderously and the Pelton wheels spun 24 hours a day.

Visitors on the Annual Tour of the Mines drive their own cars in caravans of about 20, each with a Kiwanian in the lead. Starting early in the morning and ending sometime in the afternoon, you visit at least five mines, plus the big Pelton wheel (see page 76) and the Malakoff Diggin's (see page 78). The tour fee of $3 (half price for children) includes a lunch that features a genuine Cornish pasty, a popular dish with the miners.

Even though none of the mines is operating on a commercial basis, the Kiwanis Club plans to reactivate at least one of the old vertical stamps for demonstration purposes and to open up some of the underground passages so visitors can see how the miners worked underground.

Among the mines visited are the Empire, Pennsylvania, Gold Center, North Star, and Scotia. The Empire is the biggest and best, and the photogenic ruins extend over many acres. It was also the richest in the Grass Valley area and continued production until 1956. Tunnels from this mine extend as far as the intersection of South Auburn and Main streets in downtown Grass Valley.

The Pennsylvania is adjacent to the Empire and once was part of the Empire complex. The most conspicuous ruin is the hoist machinery with its gear levers that are a source of endless fascination to children.

Machinery at the Gold Center Mine will be moved into Boston Ravine — the site of the big Pelton wheel — when the new freeway cuts through the old site. Most impressive piece of mine machinery is the big 30-stamp mill that is remarkably well preserved. Stamps such as this one were fabricated at the Miners Foundry, which is still in business in Nevada City.

The North Star is the most disappointing mine on the tour. Very little is left of the old machinery, and only mountains of tailings and a few foundations are still discernible.

Most mines are dismantled when they are closed, and most of the salvageable material is taken away. The exception to this is the Scotia Mine, one of the last mines to get going in the Grass Valley area. Because the mine has not been torn down, you can get a more accurate picture of the complex of buildings, and the relative positions of the shaft, mill, and other important points.

Timbuctoo

This once-prospering stage stop is marked by the ruins of a Wells Fargo Building. But the old structure has been so badly paint-smeared by vandals that it has lost all character.

Timbuctoo supposedly was named for an African miner who was the first to pan for gold nearby.

North San Juan

Despite its Spanish name, North San Juan was as Yankee a town as any in the Northern Diggings. It is believed to have been named San Juan by a veteran of the Mexican War who saw a resemblance to a hill in Mexico on which a prison of that name stood. "North" was tacked on when the town acquired a post office in 1857.

When San Juan Ridge's hydraulic diggin's were being worked, the town was a center for thousands, and it is still the trading center for the few hundred who remain in the area.

Brick ruins along the main street of town include the town hall and the Wells Fargo Office.

Nevada City

Some long-time visitors to this part of the country claim that the recently-completed freeway through Nevada City has done irreparable damage to the old town. They may be right. Even though very few old buildings were torn down to make way for the new highway, the mood of gracious elegance of the town has been rudely shattered by the new mass of concrete.

Away from this streak of modernity, Nevada City still manages to be one of the most charming of all the major Gold Rush towns. Its church spires, reaching high above the pine trees and roof tops on the slopes of Deer Creek Ravine, are noticeable as you first enter town. If you drive the side streets, you'll find some old commercial buildings and Victorian houses. The early-day architecture is eye-catching and memory-provoking: broad balconies and roof turrets, mullioned windows and widows' walks, garden gazebos and picket fences. If you want to explore on foot, the Nevada City Chamber of Commerce office in the City Hall sells a *Walking Tours* guidebook.

One of the earliest towns in the Northern Mines, Nevada City sprang up when miners started working the placers along Deer Creek in 1849. It was known by various names — Caldwell's Upper Store, Deer Creek Dry Diggin's, Coyoteville, and finally Nevada. The

Brick ruin on main street in North San Juan originally was built as a store, later converted to a garage.

Graceful old National Hotel (see page 81) is the centerpiece on Nevada City's Broad Street.

"City" was added later to distinguish it from the nearby territory that took the same name.

Like other Gold Rush towns, Nevada City started as a camp, then became a tent village, and then a tinderbox town of wooden buildings (in 1853). Razed by fire, it was rebuilt, burned, was rebuilt again, and burned again in 1856. It was this last conflagration that caused the citizens to form fire companies and build three good firehouses. Two are still in use by the Nevada City fire department, and the third houses the Historical Museum. Nearby is the Ott Assay Office, which barely escaped the freeway's path.

Broad Street is the main thoroughfare of town, and along it you'll find the venerable National Hotel (see page 81), the New York Hotel, Methodist Church (1864), and red brick Firehouse No. 2. Farther out, on West Broad Street, is the pioneer cemetery.

The old Chinese section was located on Commercial Street, and you'll still find a few of the buildings built in the 1860's. Coyote Street is named after the "coyote holes," small shafts used to get at the gold deposits buried deep in the gravels of old river beds. The Miners Foundry on Spring Street built the Gold Country's first Pelton wheel.

THIS IS THE WHEEL
THAT DROVE THE PISTONS
THAT POWERED THE MINES
THAT GOLD BUILT

One of the most important inventions to come out of the California Gold Rush was the Pelton wheel, a super-efficient waterwheel employing modern turbine principles to produce useful power. The inventor was Lester Pelton of Camptonville, who patented his wonderful wheel in 1878.

One of the biggest by far — and one of the last — of the great Pelton wheels is in Grass Valley at the site of the North Star Mining Company on Boston Ravine. This was the largest Pelton wheel in the world when it was installed in 1896. It is 30 feet in diameter, weighs about 10 tons, and worked for 40 years. You can imagine the strength and fine balance that had to be built into it when you realize that, at normal operating speed of 65 revolutions per minute, the rim was moving at the rate of 70 miles per hour.

The Pelton wheel was instantly recognizable by the large number of relatively small buckets affixed to the rim (most of the 60 buckets on the Grass Valley wheel are gone). Each bucket was a single casting or forging divided by a central ridge into two bowl-like scoops. A jet of water delivered from a high-pressure nozzle aimed dead center at the bucket was split by the dividing ridge and turned within the two bowls into two powerful reverse jets that drove the bucket forward.

Pelton wheels are still being manufactured in Philadelphia. They sometimes turn dynamos to generate electricity, but most mining machinery late in the last century and early in this one was powered by compressed air. Internal-combustion or steam engines in the mines would have asphyxiated the miners and water in the shafts and tunnels made the use of electric motors uncertain and hazardous. The big wheel in Boston Ravine steadily cranked the massive connecting rods of two 30-inch and two 18-inch pistons to power the hoists,

Lester Pelton's gift to the Gold Rush.

pumps, triphammers, drills, and forges of the North Star Mine, to which the compressed air was delivered through 800 feet of 6-inch pipe, at a pressure of 90 pounds per square inch.

In 1953, during a brief power shortage, an attempt was made to put the North Star's two Pelton wheels back into action, but the old water pipes would not withstand the pressure required for the nozzle. In 1959, the entire plant was sold for scrap. Salvage of the 30-foot wheel was left to the last, and on the very day the acetylene torches were slated to cut it down, an anonymous donor gave $2,000 for its purchase from the wrecking company. In 1961, the owning mining company deeded the land on which it stands to the city of Grass Valley.

In 1867, Timbuctoo was a thriving little town. Ruins of Stewart Store (next to stage) are still standing.

One of the most colorful characters in early Nevada City history (or, for that matter, all Gold Country history) was Madame Eleanore Dumont, the lady gambler. She arrived in Nevada City one day in 1854 — young, well-dressed, and of polite demeanor. But it wasn't long before the town learned of her purpose. She opened a *vignt-et-un* parlor that became the talk of the mines. Charming, proper in every way except that she was a professional gambler, Madame Dumont was a truly unique figure.

For two years she dealt the game, known also as "twenty-one" or "blackjack," to willing Nevada City miners, but as the surface deposits began to peter out, business slowed, and in 1856 Eleanore Dumont, who was to be remembered by all as Madame Moustache, moved on. The name, which followed her in later years as she traveled from camp to camp, was prompted by the dark, downy line on her upper lip, and it summed up the lack of respect that grew as the years tarnished the once-bright young woman.

No one is quite sure where Madame Moustache went. Tradition has it that she traveled all over the West from one boom town to the next, always gambling, always dealing the same game. Twenty-five years after she first stepped off the stage in Nevada City she was found dead near Bodie, a suicide.

Washington

Washington is a lumber town today, but all around the old settlement are the miniature mountains of boulders that miners a century ago piled up in their back-breaking search for gold. Two old stone buildings — one

Nevada City of 1852 was a ramshackle little camp that was easy prey to fire; later construction was more durable.

Brick firehouse on the right and the white Methodist Church on Broad Street date back to the 1860's.

Time has weathered the ugly hydraulic scars on San Juan Ridge and given them an eerie beauty.

EVOLUTION OF AN EYESORE

Between 1866 and 1884, the Malakoff Diggin's were the scene of the biggest hydraulic mining operation in the world. Today, they are the biggest mining scar to be found in all the Gold Rush Country. The Diggin's themselves have gone through quite a physical change in the century since their mining heyday, and public opinion about them has gone through a similar evolution. An eyesore has become a scenic wonder.

The early miners who first worked the gravels of San Juan Ridge recognized that there was gold in the ground. But the ore was low-grade, and it didn't pay a single miner with a pan or a small group with sluice boxes to wash tons of the gravel for only a few grains of gold. It took the large-scale hydraulic mining companies to bring the ridge into production. By tearing the gravel loose with high-pressure water systems and then washing it in a series of sluice boxes, the hydraulickers could make a profit from gravel that would yield only ten cents a cubic yard.

North Bloomfield mushroomed as soon as the hydraulicking was started, and the town had a population of

Hydraulic nozzles had devastating power.

more than 1,200 in 1880. Hundreds of men were employed getting the gold, and hundreds more worked to build and maintain a 300-mile network of flumes and canals that was needed to bring water to the hydraulic nozzles from special reservoirs in the high Sierra.

Hydraulic mining ended in 1884, but not before it had done terrible things to the land. San Juan Ridge had been re-sculptured by the hand of man. The natural slopes were gone, and in their place were miles of steep cliffs, badly gouged ravines, and acres of waste gravel. Trees and grass were gone, and only the naked rock stood in their place. The raw mountains were a disgrace, and the cause of some sadness and embarrassment. The Malakoff Diggin's were something to ignore.

But gradually, nature softened the heavy-handedness of man, and people began to come back to look at the Malakoff Diggin's as an important historical site. As the landscape became softer, it was somehow easier to forgive the men who had gouged the countryside in their greed. Water and wind rounded the steep slopes into spectacular minarets and pinnacles. Oxidized minerals tinted the gravels with color. Grass and trees grew again, and natural rain-fed lakes formed at the base of the cliffs. What was once the source of embarrassment became an object of pride and wonder.

The final exaltation of the Malakoff Diggin's came with the preservation of several thousand acres of San Juan Ridge as a state historical park, with headquarters in North Bloomfield.

According to local accounts, the name of the Diggin's can probably be interpreted as a salute to a French national hero. Jean Jacques Pelissier, a commander of French Forces in the Crimea, became a national hero because of an assault on Fort Malakoff in 1855, and he later was named the *duc de Malakoff*. Since there were many Frenchmen among the early settlers of North Bloomfield, the basis for this reasoning is probably sound.

Covered bridge at Bridgeport casts a crazy pattern of light and shadow on the old wooden roadbed.

Relief Hill may be pretty well abandoned, but the caretaker of old frame buildings still means business.

with the date 1867 carved into its keystone—once served as saloons.

North Bloomfield

Even though North Bloomfield is still inhabited and is in some ways one of the pleasantest communities in the Gold Country, there is a kind of lonely, other-world feeling that many visitors sense when they arrive. Perhaps it is the silence and complete lack of commercial activity. Or perhaps it is the proximity to the Malakoff Diggin's (see page 78).

The town was once called "Humbug," in honor of an imaginative, hard-drinking miner who lured dozens of miners to the area with his wild stories about gold-bearing gravels.

Relief Hill

It is believed that the second relief party sent out to aid the Donner party met the refugees and their rescuers near Relief Hill. Long abandoned, there are now only a couple of frame shacks to mark the site of the old town that was first settled in 1853 and had a population of 300 in 1857.

There's nothing small about the French Corral Community Center; it once served as a popular hotel.

Hotel Leger has been handsomely refurbished.   Sierra Nevada House is just north of Coloma.

A GOLD RUSH HOME AWAY FROM HOME

There is no shortage of accommodations in the Gold Country. Touring families can choose between hotels dating back 100 years or so and motels that have been in business less than a year. Though you may have to sacrifice some of the creature comforts, a night or two in one of the old-fashioned hotels can add something special to your trip into the foothills.

At least nine hotels can classify as authentic Gold Country inns. Not all of the buildings date back to the 1850's but each of the eight has managed to preserve a distinctly old-fashioned atmosphere. There are differences in the settings. Some of the hotels have elegant dining rooms for the guests; others have no kitchen and guests take their meals at nearby restaurants. Some have been refurbished in elegant Victorian style, and others maintain a comfortable simplicity with brass bedsteads, starched white curtains, and a bathroom down the hall. Some hotels have been operating for more than a century; others are in historic old buildings that have been converted to hotels in recent years.

If you've never stayed in a Gold Country inn, be sure you look at the room before you check in. The owners will not be offended, and you can decide in advance whether the character of the place suits your disposition.

Most of the hotels listed here are very popular, and advance reservations are advised, particularly on weekends and throughout the summer vacation period. Some of the inns close for short periods during the off-season or on certain days of the week. All of the towns mentioned here are covered in detail in other parts of the book; like the travel sections, the list of hotels is arranged in a south-to-north order.

GUNN HOUSE, SONORA. Gunn House was built in 1851 as a private residence for Dr. Lewis C. Gunn. It was the first two-story adobe building in the area and later served as an important community center. The hotel was opened in 1963 with 30 rooms (with private baths) refurbished in keeping with its historic past. There is a particularly handsome fireplace of unpolished marble and an antique credenza of mahogany in the sitting room. Modern touches include air conditioning and a swimming pool.

MURPHYS HOTEL, MURPHYS. The two-story hotel has welcomed such famous guests as Mark Twain, Horatio Alger, and Sir Thomas Lipton in the years since it opened in 1856. Several rooms have been refurbished in recent years; bathroom facilities are adjoining but not private. The hotel restaurant is open daily.

HOTEL LEGER, MOKELUMNE HILL. The handsome Hotel Léger reopened under new management in 1966 after having been closed for about a year. Originally called the Grand Hotel, it was built by Frenchman George Léger in 1852. In 1866, Léger purchased the adjoining county courthouse when the county seat was moved to San Andreas. The ground level area was remodeled into a General Store and hotel rooms were built above.

In 1959, the hotel was extensively remodeled and restored. Its 13 rooms, most of them with private baths, are spacious and attractively appointed with authentic Victorian furniture. There are two dining rooms and a swimming pool.

NATIONAL HOTEL, JACKSON. The National's history dates back to 1852. The present building was built in 1864, and the hotel has been in continuous operation since that time. There are 50 rooms, including 36 with private bath that have been redecorated in the decor of the mid-1800's. The hotel entrance is typical of the era it represents: It opens into the saloon. Rooms are upstairs. The Louisiana Restaurant is on a lower level.

ST. GEORGE HOTEL, VOLCANO. The St. George has been in business ever since it was built in 1862. The three-story building has wide verandas fronting the second and third floors, and trumpet vines grow clear to the rooftop. There are 14 rooms in the hotel proper, with bathrooms nearby, but not private. Rooms with private bath are in a more modern annex building. The hotel accommodations are small, comfortable, simple but attractive. There is a large, attractive lobby and a dining room. Luncheon is open to the public, but dinner is served by reservation only.

MINE HOUSE, AMADOR CITY. The Mine House opened as a motel in 1955 in a building that had housed offices of the Keystone Mine for more than a hundred years. It has eight rooms (with private baths) that are furnished authentically in the style of the 1850's. The rooms are named in keeping with their former use, and in some it's still apparent: The Vault, for example, still retains heavy doors in an interior wall. Other rooms — Retort, Assay, Stores, Grinding, Directors, Bookkeeping, Keystone — refer to other activities formerly carried on here. Mine House has no restaurant, and guests usually eat in Sutter Creek or Jackson. There is a swimming pool.

SIERRA NEVADA HOUSE III, COLOMA. This is a replica of a Gold Rush Hotel, and its nine rooms (with private baths) have decor and appointments in the style of 1849. There is an old-fashioned soda parlor and candy department, and a Victorian dining room that serves lunch and dinner by reservation only. Room rates include breakfast. One of the grandest gold scales ever seen in the Gold Country is on display in the lobby. It was originally purchased to weigh the vast quantities of gold produced by the Pacific Mine above Placerville.

THE RED CASTLE, NEVADA CITY. Once a proud home and center of the social life of Nevada City, the Red Castle has been restored and refitted in frontier Victorian antiques. Rates for upstairs guest suites, or guest room sharing sitting room and bath, include morning coffee and afternoon tea.

NATIONAL HOTEL, NEVADA CITY. The National Hotel, a three-story balconied building on the main street of town, has been open since 1856. It has 25 rooms with private baths, all refurbished with handsome Victorian furnishings and decor, plus some new motel-type units. There is an attractively appointed dining room that serves lunch and dinner, and a swimming pool.

Gunn House was an early Sonora residence.

Amador City's Mine House is authentically furnished.

National Hotel in Nevada City opened in 1863.

Remote town of Cherokee has as many legends about diamond mining as it does about gold prospecting. But the diamonds never made anybody rich, and the gold mining kept the town going for more than 30 years.

THE OROVILLE AREA

OROVILLE • CHEROKEE • RICH BAR • FORBESTOWN • WOODLEAF

STRAWBERRY VALLEY • LAPORTE • GIBSONVILLE • HOWLAND FLAT

Oroville

From 1849 through the early 1900's, Oroville was a vigorous mining town. The placers were first worked by hand, then by hydraulic mining until it was outlawed, and finally by dredging operations. The ancient river bed on which Oroville is built is so rich in gold that a dredging company once offered to move the whole town just for the right to mine the ground on which it stood.

Thousands of acres of waste tailings left over from the days when dredgers worked the river bottoms were used in the construction of the Oroville Dam, thereby eliminating an eyesore from the landscape and putting the historic old gravels to a useful purpose.

Today, unless you stop and look carefully, you will see little more than a hint of Oroville's gold boom.

The quiet, tree-shaded town has a dual economic base — the tremendous water projects on the branches of the Feather River, and the thousands of acres of olive, citrus, and deciduous fruit orchards that thrive in the mild climate.

Perhaps the most interesting visit you can make in Oroville is to the Chinese Temple on Broderick Street. This is all that remains of the sizable Chinese community that once flourished in Oroville in the 1870's. Built in 1863, the temple buildings now house extensive displays of tapestries, lamps, gongs, carvings, shrines, sedan chairs, and other magnificent museum pieces. An auxiliary building was erected in 1967 to provide additional space for draperies that were contributed by descendants of the original Chinese colony.

Another valuable stop is the Pioneer and Relics

Beautiful Chinese Temple in Oroville houses a dazzling display of religious shrines and artifacts.

Masonic Hall in Forbestown has been in use since 1857. All other Gold Rush buildings are gone.

Building, where early-day tools and implements are on display. The best-preserved residence in town is the C. F. Lott Home on Montgomery Street. The home was built in the 1850's, and today serves as a museum for period furnishings and displays of photographs.

Cherokee

This area was the scene of extensive hydraulic mining operations, and in the year 1870 alone, produced about $5 million in gold. Some 7,000 people lived in town at that time, and the great hydraulic nozzles ate huge

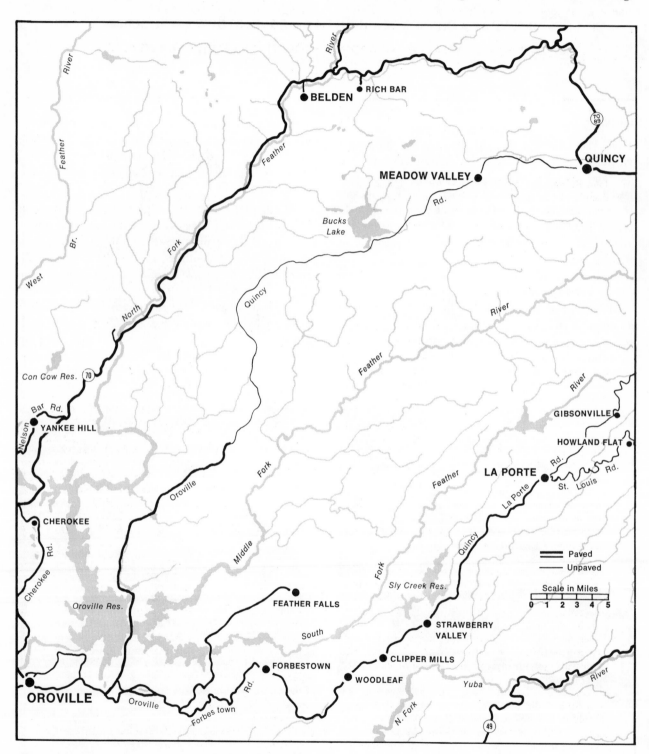

Forks of the Feather River are popular vacation spots. Oroville-Quincy Road is unpaved in center section. The old stage route through Forbestown and Strawberry Valley is paved as far as LaPorte.

chunks out of the nearby hills; the great scar on Table Mountain is still visible for miles.

The Anti-Debris Act of 1883 ended the hydraulicking and dealt the town a death blow; by 1906, all organized gold mining had ceased and Cherokee became a ghost town. The ruins of the Spring Valley Assay Office and an old hotel converted into a museum are the only remaining historical structures.

The first diamonds ever discovered in the United States were picked out of a Cherokee sluice box in 1866. There were many stories about miners finding big gems, and even a far-fetched tale about a fortunate woman who found a two-carat stone in the craw of a Christmas turkey that allegedly had spent its youth in Cherokee. But no company ever made a success out of diamond mining in the region, so most of the stories have to be assigned to the realm of mining legend until some new evidence can be produced.

A MAN TO MATCH THE MOUNTAINS

John Bidwell was one of the most enterprising and productive of the California pioneers. A self-made man who came West in 1841, Bidwell played a major role in the early settlement of northern California and in the development of its agriculture, commerce, and politics. His contributions to the Gold Rush were secondary to other interests, but nonetheless very important in the overall scheme of things.

Bidwell actually had the chance to beat James Marshall to his discovery of gold by four years. In 1844, he was working as manager of John Sutter's hock farm. One of the Mexican farm workers, Pablo Gutierrez, approached Bidwell one day and told him that there was gold to be dug on the Bear River. Bidwell went with the Mexican into the hills and actually did see some flecks of gold on the river bed. But Gutierrez insisted that the gold could not be taken in any quantity without a *batea,* which was available only in Mexico. Bidwell did not want to finance a trip to get the *batea,* so the gold mining was postponed for lack of the proper equipment. What Bidwell did not realize was that a *batea* was nothing more than a shallow dish and was easily obtainable in California.

Bidwell subsequently became involved with other important matters and was unable to devote any more time to the gold. Within four years, however, he was to see thriving mining camps on the very spot where he and Gutierrez had first spotted gold.

Even though Bidwell missed this first opportunity, he was quick to realize the importance of Marshall's discovery at Coloma. Bidwell was in Chico in January, 1848, but heard about the gold when he visited Sutter's Fort in February. Bidwell was on his way to the San Francisco area for supplies, and he spread the news on the way. When his business was completed, Bidwell made a hurried trip to Coloma to look over the terrain, and was immediately impressed by its resemblance to the Feather River country.

On his way back to Chico, Bidwell camped on the west bank of the Feather River. He found a few flecks of gold in the sand and rightly assumed that there was more at higher elevations. At Chico, he organized a scouting party and started prospecting on the middle fork of the Feather. Within a short time, he made a big

Bidwell often led the way.

strike at Bidwell's Bar (now submerged under the waters of the Oroville Dam reservoir). The date of the discovery is usually given as July 4, but Bidwell's biographers place it much earlier in the spring.

The mining camp at Bidwell's Bar grew into a rich little town, and served as county seat from 1853 until the gold gave out in 1856. Bidwell himself evidently made a great deal of money in a short time as a miner and operator of a trading post, and then abandoned mining forever in 1850 to return to his first love, agriculture. He already owned a ranch on Chico Creek, and his new riches enabled him to get another piece of land known as Rancho Chico. Within a few years, Bidwell was recognized as the most noted agriculturalist in California, and he pioneered in the manufacture of wine and olive oil.

Between 1848 and his death in 1900, Bidwell became a very influential public figure, and served in both the state Senate and the U. S. House of Representatives. He was twice a candidate for state governor, and the Prohibition party candidate for President in 1892. He was the "father" of the city of Chico and donated land for Chico State College as part of his vigorous campaign for better education in the state. He served as one of the early regents of the University of California, was a great friend of the California Indians, and was one of the first proponents of the transcontinental railway.

He may have missed out as the discoverer of gold in Northern California, but John Bidwell has a secure and honorable place in history for his other, more valuable contributions to the West.

Rich Bar

This was the scene of the richest gold strike in the Feather River country. Two Germans stumbled across Rich Bar quite by acicdent in 1850, and after taking $2,900 in their first two pans, they decided to stick around. The lucky partners managed to get more than $30,000 out before the place was overrun with new miners. The gravel turned out to be so rich that each claim was limited to 10 square feet. The total take was something between $14 and $23 million.

Rich Bar enjoyed an exciting life, but it was a brief one. Within six years, the gravels had been worked out and the miners had disappeared over the hills in search of another dream.

Forbestown

Forbestown was founded in 1850 by B. F. Forbes and was part of the mining scene for about 50 years. The only reminder is the restored Masonic Hall, built in 1857 and now home of the second oldest Masonic lodge in California.

Woodleaf

This tiny settlement was founded by Charles Barker in 1850 and was first known as Barker's Ranch. James Wood took over the place in the late 1850's and built the Woodville House, which is still the biggest landmark for miles.

"THE BOLDEST ROBBERY EVER CHRONICLED"

Dr. Thomas J. Hodges was one of the most unlikely bad guys ever to roam the Gold Rush Country. A meek man who hated guns and bloodshed, Dr. Hodges enjoyed only a few years of notoriety and would have been relegated to a secondary role in the history of California except for one feat. He was the first person ever to rob a stagecoach. "Tom Bell, the Highwayman," Dr. Hodges called himself, and under this fierce misnomer, he opened a new era in the history of Western crime.

How Thomas J. Hodges became Tom Bell is a curious story. The young doctor first practiced in his home town of Rome, Tennessee, and then served as a medical attache with the Tennessee Volunteers during the War with Mexico. When the fighting was over he came West. But for some reason, the doctor abandoned medicine. He tried mining, then gambling, and finally thievery, but wasn't very successful at any of them. It was after his arrest as a bandit in 1855 that Hodges took a new name. While casting around for some pseudonym that would keep his real name off the prison roles, he remembered hearing of a small-time crook named Tom Bell, who operated around Auburn. This sounded like a logical connection, so Hodges took the name of Tom Bell.

Bell, nee Hodges, broke out of prison very shortly in the company of Bill Gristy, a roughneck bandit. The two of them stayed together and quickly assembled a gang of versatile outlaws that committed burglary, cattle thievery, holdups, and other crimes throughout the Northern Mines.

Bell, himself, apparently did not like to shoot people and loot stores. But he was an organizer. The gang split up into small teams, and often struck simultaneously at widely scattered points. All the members of the gang identified themselves as "Tom Bell" to the victims, thereby confusing the law. So successful was this gambit, Bell might never have been caught if it hadn't been for the famous stage holdup.

Bell apparently decided to rob the Marysville-Camptonville stage in the summer of 1856 just to show he could do something spectacular. The date selected was August 11, when the stage would be carrying $100,000 in gold. Bell and five of his gang set up a perfect ambush near Dry Creek, just outside of Marysville, and waited. But an unexpected horseman rode into the ambush, and three of the robbers had to get him out of the way.

While they were occupied elsewhere, the stagecoach arrived. Bell had no choice but to try and stop it with only two helpers. It wasn't enough. The armed messenger riding in the shotgun seat killed one of the bandits and engaged the other two in a furious gunfight while the stage driver rode through the blockade. The messenger was wounded, one passenger (a woman) was killed, and two others were injured. The stagecoach made it on to Marysville, and Tom Bell was in trouble.

The robbery caused a great uproar. Said one newspaper, "This is the boldest robbery ever chronicled." Posses searched the countryside, and Tom Bell ran. He escaped the Northern Mines, and tried to hole up at a friend's ranch near Knights Ferry. A posse caught up with one of Tom's men and after a night-long session of "questioning" he revealed Tom's hideout. The daring bandit was quietly captured on October 4.

Tom was strung up by the men who nabbed him, but not before he made a full confession of his crimes and wrote a letter to his mother. The letter carried a poignant message of repentance and ended, ". . . Give my respects to all of my old and youthful friends. Tell them to beware of bad associations, and never to enter into any gambling saloons, for that has been my ruin.

"If my old grandmother is living, remember me to her. With these remarks I bid you farewell forever.

Your only boy, Tom"

Though Tom Bell failed in his attempt to rob a stagecoach, he planted the idea in the minds of many other men who were more adept as highwaymen. They learned from Tom's mistake and soon developed more efficient schemes that enabled them to plunder the stagecoach companies for decades.

THE LETTERS OF DAME SHIRLEY

The '49ers and their followers were pretty good at letter-writing. Often separated from family and friends, the miners relieved their homesickness and frustrations with long letters to folks back home. Any good-sized public library contains at least a few collections of these letters, preserved as eye-witness accounts of early California. Unfortunately, many of these letters are not very perceptive, and dwell on inconsequential gossip and uninspired comments about climate and the loneliness of life in the mines.

The exception to this pattern are the letters written from Rich Bar by one of the few women of breeding and taste who came to California during the first few years of the Gold Rush. She was Mrs. Louise Amelia Knapp Smith Clappe, "Dame Shirley" to her friends. Dame Shirley spent only one year (1851-52) in the mines, but that was enough time for her to write a couple of dozen letters back to her sister in "the states." These letters,

published many times and available in book form (*The Shirley Letters,* Alfred A. Knopf, 1949) are the best first-hand accounts of life in this turbulent period.

Shirley was married to Dr. Fayette Clappe, who came to California from the East for his health and decided to settle in the mining town of Rich Bar rather than San Francisco because of reports he had heard about the bracing mountain air and invigorating climate. Dr. Clappe lasted only a year at Rich Bar, and his career there was undistinguished except for the letter-writing of his observant wife, who was able to put her thoughts down on paper with wit and style.

Dr. and Mrs. Clappe returned to San Francisco and eventually were divorced. When her health failed, Dame Shirley returned to the East and died in 1906 at the age of 87. Fortunately for modern readers, the letters of Dame Shirley live on, painting a vivid picture of a time and place that is very hard to keep in focus.

Strawberry Valley

There is some confusion about the origin of this town's name — either it came from the profusion of wild berries that grew in the area, or it is the combination of the names of two early miners, Straw and Berry.

At any rate, Strawberry Valley was a commercial center for the many mines that sprouted into life in the surrounding valleys during the 1850's. At one time, there were dozens of stores and hotels. Now, only the Columbus Hotel (still with its original well) stands by the side of the main road.

La Porte

La Porte was a well-populated hydraulic mining center before the Anti-Debris Act was passed, but now it is a small mountain town with only the crumbling Wells Fargo Office Building and the Union Hotel as reminders of the good old days.

Gibsonville and Howland Flat

This rugged section of mountains was settled in 1850. Gibsonville, perched on a windswept ridge overlooking Slate Creek, was named for one of the early prospectors. Only a few bleached houses mark the site.

Howland Flat was one of the most populous camps in the Northern Mines for a short time because of its rich hydraulic diggings. The site of Poker Flat — the scene of Bret Harte's most famous story — can be reached via a three-mile trail from Howland Flat.

Small settlements such as Woodleaf dot the remote Sierra country between the Feather and Yuba rivers.

Hydraulic mining built LaPorte, and the Anti-Debris Act of 1883 caused the collapse of the community.

Modern-day prospectors work the Middle Fork of the Yuba River at Foote's Crossing. Skin diver uses an underwater sluice to capture heavy gravels, which are then panned out by second man working on shore.

THE DOWNIEVILLE AREA

CAMPTONVILLE • GOODYEARS BAR • FOREST • ALLEGHENY
DOWNIEVILLE • SIERRA CITY • JOHNSVILLE

Camptonville

Camptonville, named for pioneer blacksmith Robert Campton, is a town that twice survived the attack of hydraulic monitors by moving each time before its foundations were washed away. Gold was found here in 1852, but real prosperity came only after hydraulic mining started in the late 1860's.

You'll find two monuments side by side on the west end of town. One is erected to the memory of Lester Pelton, inventor of the Pelton wheel which was so important in the development of hydroelectric power equipment (see page 76).

The other was dedicated by E Clampus Vitus to William "Bull" Meek — who, the marker reads, was

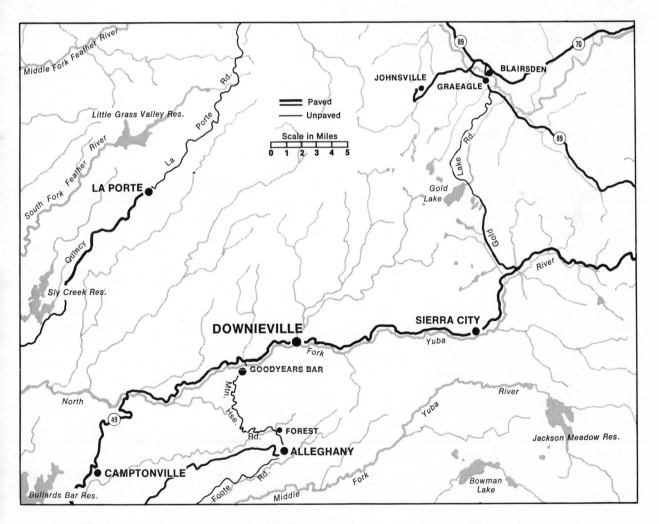

Forest and Allegheny are accessible by dirt road out of Goodyears Bar, or the scary but spectacular Foote's Crossing Road out of North Columbia. At 4,187 feet, Sierra City is the highest town on Highway 49.

The town flourished only until a bigger strike was made on the south side of Pliocene Ridge. Within a few years of the new discovery, Forest's population had moved to Allegheny.

A few of the old buildings are still standing, including a tobacco and confectionery shop, and a weathered Catholic church.

Allegheny

Allegheny is built on the bias. The houses balance precariously on side hill terraces, and look as if they might fall into the ravine at any minute. The streets are narrow and wind down from one level to the next.

At the bottom of the ravine is Kanaka Creek, named after the Hawaiians who made the first big strike in May of 1850. Kanaka Creek was rich in gold and brought a real boom to the primitive mountain country.

The most famous of Allegheny's mines was the Original 16-to-1 mine. It was opened in 1896 and provided the economic backbone of the community until the 1960's. In 1966, the mine had to be closed and sold. The equipment was stripped in 1967 and only a few boarded-up buildings can be seen today.

Downieville

Fire and flood have done their best to destroy this mountain settlement, but Downieville is still one of the most entrancing gold towns left. The old stone, brick, and frame buildings, many of which were built in the 1860's or earlier, face on quiet, crooked streets that once echoed with the clatter and rumble of freighters and the din that hundreds, sometimes thousands, of miners could raise when they came to town for relaxation and a cup to slake their thirst. The town was named for Major William Downie who wintered here in 1849.

Like many other camps along the forks of the Yuba, Downieville has contributed its share of true stories of rich strikes — like that of Tin Cup Diggings where three miners had little trouble filling a cup with dust each day, or of the 60-square-foot claim that gave up over $12,000 in eleven days, or of the 25-pound nugget of solid gold taken two miles above the camp.

There are several buildings that are almost as old as the stories. On the main street of town are the present-day museum with walls of schist, the Costa store, and the two-story Craycroft Building with its iron doors. On the south side of the river, the Masonic Building, the Native Daughters Hall across the street,

Remote and quiet, Forest now gives no hint of its lively existence during the early 1850's.

"Stage Driver — Wells Fargo Agent — Teamster — Merchant."

Meek is believed to be the only regular stage driver in all the area never to have been robbed by holdup men. Some old-timers will tell you that he escaped being robbed because he regularly carried supplies to a Downieville bordello. According to this theory, the madam and her ladies used their influence on the region's badmen to keep their contact with the rest of the world safe.

Goodyears Bar

This crossing on the Yuba River was named for the brothers Andres and Miles Goodyear, who settled here in 1849 with a few friends. The camp boomed in 1852 after word got around that $2,000 was taken from a single wheelbarrow load of dirt. But the good times were short lived, and there is very little left today except a few frame buildings and a sparse population.

Forest

Once a lively camp in the 1850's, Forest is now a quiet little mountain town with only a handful of residents.

Downieville museum is housed in a stone building erected in 1852; it is just as solid today as when it opened.

Main street in Downieville still has a distinct mountain character that is reminiscent of the Gold Rush.

the Catholic Church and the Methodist Church all date from the 1850's and 1860's.

A few blocks east of the museum, the site of Downie's original cabin is marked. Over by the courthouse is the original town gallows, built in 1885 to hang James O'Neal.

Many other buildings which were built in the 1860's cling to the mountainsides above the river. The lovely old residential section adds to the charm which makes Downieville a favorite with tourists.

But it wasn't always quaint and quiet.

Downieville has the dubious distinction of being the only camp in the Gold Country to have hanged a woman. The story is clouded, and even early newspaper accounts take violently opposing views of the lynching.

Most historians now believe that Juanita, the fiery Mexican dance hall girl who plunged a knife into the breast of an annoying miner named Jack Cannon, acted in self-defense and was wrongfully lynched. At the time, other miners claimed that the stabbing was unprovoked and that she got what she deserved when they hauled her up on the hastily-built gallows. No one will ever know whether she was actually with child as she claimed before they strung her up, or whether this would have made any difference to the

Photo taken in 1861 shows Downieville after a flood. Despite repeated fires and floods, the town still prospers.

Biggest reminder of the mining days in Sierra City is the Busch Building on the main highway.

Mining complex at Plumas-Eureka State Park is undergoing a gradual restoration to its original condition.

mob. Right or wrong, the news electrified California and made news around the world.

Another story, often told, strikes a humorous vein. It seems that in 1850 a rascal was caught with a pair of stolen boots. The miners quickly gathered to hold court in the business place of the justice of the peace — a saloon. The culprit's guilt was established, but instead of a flogging or worse, he was ordered to buy the house drinks. After several rounds, the guilty one went unnoticed as he quietly slipped out the door taking with him Exhibit A, the boots, and leaving behind the bill for the drinks.

Sierra City

The towering Sierra Buttes overshadow the mountain town of Sierra City. Miners punctured these dramatic granite peaks with tunnels and shafts between 1850 and 1852 following the discovery of a quartz ledge. But the mountains had their revenge in 1852 when an avalanche of ice and snow crushed every shack and tent in the boom town that had mushroomed because of the rich deposits.

Most of the old structures left in town date from

the 1870's; the biggest is the Busch Building which was built in 1871. Wells Fargo was one of the early tenants.

Johnsville

The best-preserved wood-constructed town in the Northern Mines is Johnsville, in the center of Plumas-Eureka State Park. As a mining camp, Johnsville is a latecomer, having been built in the 1870's by a company of London investors who bought up land in the vicinity.

There are several old buildings in various stages of collapse, and the spot is an excellent one for photographers. Tourists are advised to tread carefully, however, since most of the buildings are privately owned.

Plumas-Eureka State Park has a good collection of old mining implements and wagons, and the state is working on a long-range program to restore the stamp mill of the Plumas-Eureka Mine and some of the other surface buildings.

An old boarding house from the mining days has been transformed into the park headquarters and museum. Here, you can see tools and hand-made mining equipment that were in common use during the nineteenth century.

THE TIME OF THE ARGONAUTS—A CHRONOLOGY

It is often difficult to keep the big picture of the California Gold Rush in mind as you travel along Highway 49. Each town offers but a small bit of history, and the grand scheme of things tends to get lost in a morass of dates, names, and details about building booms and fires. The chronology printed here is intended to help solve this problem and provide a general reference guide for your travels through the Gold Rush Country.

Because of space limitations, some discoveries and events have been omitted; but enough is included to give you a general idea of how the Gold Rush spread through California. Greatest emphasis is placed on the years 1848 to 1851, since this was the primary period of discovery.

Notable political events also are listed to put the Gold Rush in proper perspective with the development of California as a territory and a state. Additional details are readily available in any of the well-written histories of the state.

1839 August. Swiss-born John Sutter arrives at the confluence of the Sacramento and American rivers to start northern California's first inland settlement.

1841 November 4. The first California pioneers, organized by John Bidwell, arrive in the San Joaquin Valley after leaving Independence, Missouri, on May 19.

1842 March. While digging onions to eat for lunch, rancher Francisco Lopez finds gold in the San Fernando Hills, about 45 miles north of Los Angeles. Within two months, about 100 miners are working the placers. But the supply is limited and when John Bidwell visits the site in 1845, he finds about 30 miners working hard for 30 cents a day.

1842 August. General Manuel Micheltorena, the last of the Mexican governors, takes office in Monterey.

1845 March. Micheltorena is driven from the state by *Californios,* who fight among themselves for power.

1845 July. James Marshall arrives at Sutter's Fort on a wagon train from Oregon.

1846 March. Supposedly acting on orders from President Polk, Captain John C. Fremont raises the American Flag on a peak in the Salinas Valley. The gesture is ineffective.

1846 May 13. War begins between the U.S. and Mexico.

1846 June 14. Believing that the *Californios* are going to run them out of the state, a group of American ranchers ride into Sonoma, capture General Mariano Vallejo, and declare the Bear Flag Republic.

1846 July 7. Commodore John Sloat lands the U. S. Pacific Fleet at Monterey, raises the American Flag and proclaims California is part of the United States. Two days later, the U. S. flag replaces the Bear Flag at Sonoma and is raised on Yerba Buena Island.

1846 October. The first storms of what will be an exceptionally heavy winter trap the immigrant train led by George Donner in the high Sierra. By spring, 39 of the 87 members of the train will be dead of cold and starvation in the greatest tragedy of the California migration.

1847 January 13. The war in California is ended as Captain Fremont and General Pico, leader of the *Californios,* sign the Cahuenga Capitulation.

1847 Late January. The Mormon Battalion—300 recruits from Utah—arrive to fight in the War with Mexico. They are too late for the fighting, but some decide to stay and work for John Sutter.

1847 February 10. John Fremont becomes the owner of a big tract of land near Mariposa which appears worthless at the time but will ultimately become the richest in the Southern Mines.

1847 May 16. At Sutter's instruction, James Marshall sets out for the foothills to select a site for a sawmill. Marshall selects a valley on the American River that the Indians call *Culluma.*

1847 August 27. Sutter and Marshall sign an agreement to build the mill, with Sutter to provide the manpower (primarily members of the Mormon Battalion) and Marshall the know-how. Work begins in September.

1848 January 24. While examining the tailrace of the partially completed sawmill, Marshall notices something glittering in the rocks. He picks up a small piece of metal and after a few preliminary tests decides that he has found some gold.

1848 January 28. Marshall arrives in Sutter's Fort with his precious metal. Sutter subjects it to several more tests and proves conclusively that Marshall has discovered gold.

1848 February 2. The treaty of Guadalupe Hidalgo is signed and the California territory is formally ceded to the United States.

1848 February 6. Although they are pledged to secrecy about Marshall's discovery, the workers at the mill become the first Argonauts by sneaking off to pry gold nuggets out of the rock with penknives.

1848 Mid-February. Sutter sends Charles Bennett on a secret mission to Monterey to secure land rights at Coloma. But Bennett cannot keep the discovery of gold to himself and spreads the word to everyone he meets.

1848 March. Mormon Island becomes the first mining camp outside of Coloma. Sutter reports that he is losing all of his staff to the gold fields.

1848 March 11. The sawmill is finished. It will be operated sporadically for about five years before being torn down by miners who need the lumber for new buildings.

1848 March 15. The first story of the gold discovery is printed in a San Francisco newspaper, but not many people pay any attention to the report.

1848 Late March. John Bidwell visits Coloma and decides there must be gold in the northern mountains. He makes a big strike at Bidwell's Bar in April.

1848 April 1. San Francisco sends a special messenger to the East Coast with news of the rumored discovery.

1848 May. By now, 800 miners are working at Coloma, Mormon Island, Kelseys Diggings, and other areas on both sides of Sutter's Mill. One of the richest strikes of all is made at Dry Diggin's, which will ultimately become Placerville, and gold is discovered on the Yuba River near Long Barn. Claud Chana and a group of miners make a strike at North Fork, Dry Diggin's—later to become Auburn. George Angel builds a trading post on Calaveritas Creek and Angels Camp is born. Drytown is settled. After early skepticism, San Franciscans are finally convinced that gold really has been found and the rush to the foothills begins.

1848 June 1. The number of miners now working the foothills is estimated at 2,000.

1848 June 14. The last of the San Francisco newspapers suspends operation for lack of readers, and practically all business in the city is suspended.

1848 June 20. A special messenger arrives in Monterey with a pocketful of nuggets dug near Coloma. Residents are finally convinced of Marshall's discovery and make a mass exodus.

1848 June 24. A newspaper in Hawaii reports the discovery, and the first ships loaded with Argonauts leave in July.

1848 July. Some 4,000 miners are now working in the foothills. Col. R. B. Mason, Military Governor of California, visits Coloma and confirms the richness of the diggings. News of the discovery reaches Los Angeles and the first miners start north. John Sutter and a crew of Indians find gold at Sutter Creek, and John and Daniel Murphy start the town that is to carry their name.

1848 August. First rumors reach the East Coast, but there is no official confirmation yet. A Chilean ship reaches Valparaiso with the news, and several thousand men start immediately for California. Ships from Hawaii bring the news to Oregon, and wagon trains start south. New mining camps spring up at Jackson, Woods Crossing, Tuttletown, Fiddletown, and Timbuctoo. Friendly Indians lead James Carson to gold on Carson Creek. Sonorian Camp

(Sonora) becomes the southernmost mining camp to be settled in 1848.

1848 September. Heat and sickness in the mines causes some of the weaker men to abandon the diggings and return to the valleys, many settling around Sutter's Fort. Washington, D. C., receives official confirmation of Marshall's discovery.

1848 October. The number of miners has grown to 8,000. Mexico learns of the discovery, and a great migration is prepared for the following spring.

1848 November. Mokelumne Hill is founded. Rain and cold force more miners out of the hills, and only the hardy remain to continue working through the winter. On the East Coast, the first ships loaded with Argonauts leave for California and more get ready to sail from New York, Boston, Salem, Norfolk, Philadelphia, and Baltimore.

1848 December 5. President Polk's message to Congress confirms the California gold discovery. His message is backed up by a box filled with gold dust that is put on public display. The fever takes hold. Buffeted by the turn of events, James Marshall and John Sutter sell most of their interests in Coloma.

1848 December 23. A newspaper in Sydney, Australia, publishes news of the discovery; hundreds of miners set sail.

1849 January. Five California trading and mining companies are started in London, and all Europe begins to send ships loaded with miners.

1849 February 28. The steamship *California*—the first of the Pacific Mail steamers—arrives in San Francisco with the first load of '49ers.

1849 Spring. Prospecting starts again. Gold is discovered at Jacksonville, mining begins at Jenny Lind and Forest Hill, and Goodyears Bar is settled by Miles Goodyear.

1849 May. The great procession of overland wagon trains begins from St. Joseph and Independence. Some 4,000 miners from Sonora, Mexico, are on their way north.

1849 July. The first of the overland wagon trains arrives in the Sacramento Valley. By now, 600 vessels have arrived in San Francisco Bay, and both crews and passengers head immediately for the mines.

1849 September. The first miners work the gravels at Downieville; the town is started in November by Major Downie.

1849 October. The first of the European emigrants begin to arrive. Dr. A. B. Caldwell builds a general store on Deer Creek and Nevada City is born. Chinese Camp is settled, James Savage begins mining at Big Oak Flat, and the first miners set up camp at Coulterville, French Corral, Volcano, San Andreas, Groveland, Shaws Flat, and Oroville.

1849 November 13. A state constitution is ratified, a Governor is elected and senators and assemblymen are named—even though the California territory is not legally a state.

1849 Winter. It is estimated that 42,000 Argonauts have arrived by land during the year, and another 39,000 have come by sea from all parts of the world. Heavy rains force many miners out of the hills and into Sacramento and San Francisco. Their presence prompts the cities to realize their inadequacies and promotes improvements such as paved streets, sidewalks, and sewers.

1850 Spring. In the Southern Mines, Mount Bullion is settled and the first private mint in California opens at Mt. Ophir.

1850 March. Mexicans discover gold a few miles north of Sonora. On March 27 a group of American miners do the same thing, and the rush is started at Columbia.

1850 April. Yankee dislike for foreigners results in the legislative adoption of a Foreign Miners Tax of $20 a month, renewable every month. It is supposedly leveled against all "furriners" but is enforced chiefly against the Spanish-Americans and the Chinese.

1850 June. An accidental discovery of gold-bearing quartz on Gold Hill starts the rush to Grass Valley.

1850 Summer. Kanaka Creek below Allegheny is first mined by Hawaiians. A new settlement grows at Growlersburg (Georgetown), and mining starts in Onion Valley near LaPorte. Michigan Bluff and Sierra City have their first success; Washington is founded as Indian Camp.

1850 September 9. California is admitted into the Union as the 31st state.

1850 October 18. The steamer *Oregon* brings the news of statehood to San Francisco.

1850 Winter. During this year, 55,000 people have arrived on the overland caravans, and another 36,000 have come by sea.

1851 February. The first quartz mine in Amador County is discovered at Amador Creek. This, plus the findings at Grass Valley, start a big boom in quartz mining.

1851 March 14. The Foreign Miners Tax is repealed—at least temporarily.

1851 April. Gold is discovered in Australia, and the tide of Argonauts across the Pacific is reversed. Virtually all of the main California gold fields are settled by now, and prospectors must move on to find new diggings. When gold is discovered in Oregon's Rogue River country, more miners give up California in search of greener pastures.

1852 May 4. A new license fee of $3 (later to be raised to $4) is assessed against all foreign miners.

1852 Summer. Mining starts at La Grange and Camptonville.

1853 March. E. E. Matteson first forces water under pressure through a nozzle to wash a gravel bank, and hydraulic mining is born.

1853 Summer. Lola Montez settles in Grass Valley; Christian Kientz discovers gold at North San Juan. Michael Savage begins mining at Forest Hill. Iowa Hill becomes a boom town. After a time of depression, confidence is restored in quartz mining that will last for decades.

1854 Spring. Bret Harte arrives in California for a 17-year stay, most of which is spent far from the mines. But his brief experiences with frontiersmen provide enough material.

1854 Summer. Lotta Crabtree gives her first performance for the miners at LaPorte and is launched on a long and successful stage career.

1854 Fall. Gold is discovered on the Kern River, drawing more miners out of northern California. Still others sail for Peru, but the stories of rich mines there turn out to be only rumors.

1855 January. Snowshoe Thompson makes his first trip across the Sierra in winter to start a unique career as one of the most remarkable postmen in history.

1855 August 11. Tom Bell attempts the first stage robbery for gold, but he is foiled and ultimately captured.

1855 October 25. The great tong war is held at Chinese Camp.

1859 July 1. The *Nevada Journal* in Nevada City publishes the results of assays of ore specimens brought from the state of Nevada, which show that silver as well as gold has been discovered. The great rush to the Comstock begins. Many historians regard this as the official end of the California Gold Rush.

1860 April 13. The first westbound rider of the Pony Express reaches San Francisco after leaving St. Joseph, Missouri, on April 3.

1861 Summer. Mark Twain arrives in the West. He will stay until 1865 and write some of the best of all the Gold Country stories.

1862 Winter. Unprecedented storms produce terrible floods that badly damage river communities and illustrate how unrestricted hydraulic mining chokes the river beds.

1877 Summer. Black Bart stages his first successful holdup.

1880 June 18. John Sutter dies in Pennsylvania.

1884 January 23. The Sawyer Decision following passage of the Anti-Debris Act of 1883 closes all the hydraulic mines in California.

1885 August 10. James Marshall dies at Kelsey.

1893 Summer. The Caminetti Act permits hydraulic mines to reopen if debris dams are built to catch all of the silt before it can clog the rivers. A few attempts are made to meet the requirements, but the cost is too great and hydraulic mining is abandoned completely.

INDEX